HYDROPONICS FOR BEGINNERS

THE DEFINITIVE BEGINNER'S GUIDE TO QUICKLY START TO GROW FRUITS, HERBS AND VEGETABLES HYDROPONICALLY AT HOME!
A PRECISE GUIDE ON HOME TECHNIQUES, AQUAPONICS, AND HYDROPONICS

Contents

Introduction 5
Chapter 1.   What is Hydroponics? 8
   Why Develop Things Hydroponically? 9
Chapter 2.   Advantages and Disadvantages 12
Chapter 3.   Equipment's 20
   Monitoring Equipment 20
      pH meter 20
      EC meter 22
      TDS meter 25
      Dissolved oxygen sensor 26
   Humidity And Temperature Sensor 29
   Germination Tray And Dome 30
   Seed Starter Cubes 31
      Rockwool cubes 32
      Coco Coir 33
      Oasis cubes 34
      Sponges 35
      Hydro ton 36
      Perlite 39
      Vermiculite 41
      Rockwool 42
      Grow stones 44
      River rock 45
Chapter 4.   Lighting and Heat 47
   Natural Lights 52
   Artificial Lights 53
Chapter 5.   Hydroponics Grow System 58

Wick Hydroponic System 58
    Materials 58
    Wicks 59
    Reservoir 61
    Directions 61
Water Culture Systems 62
    Materials 62
    Aeration Types 64
    Recirculating the System 65
    Directions 66
Ebb & Flow System 68
    Materials: 68
    Directions 69
Chapter 6. Different Types of Hydroponics Garden 73
Chapter 7. Best Plants for Hydroponics 83
Chapter 8. Nutrient Solutions 98
Chapter 9. Nutrient 112
Chapter 10. Most common Problems 119
   Starting Your Garden Without Proper Knowledge 128
   Harvesting Too Early 128
   Overwatering/Under Watering 128
   Improper Lighting 129
Chapter 11. Strategies to avoid insects 131
Chapter 12. Safeguards 142
   Algae And Fungi 142
   Water Microbes 144
   Pests And Diseases 145
   Common Solution: 147
Conclusion 152

Introduction

If we want to become hydroponic gardeners, the first thing we need to do is understand what options are available to us. This way we can choose a method that has advantages and disadvantages that are properly in line with what we are looking for. This means, for example, if we don't want to risk clogs, we could avoid using methods that involve pumps. However, if we live in an area where we have a hard time controlling the amount of light in our environment, we might find ourselves looking to a system that uses a pump rather than one of the simpler ones like a deep-water culture in which light regulation is also important.

Each of these systems offers unique advantages and disadvantages from which we can choose. But this does not mean that one particular system is better than another. Like most things in life, the choice of which hydroponic system to use should be based on your schedule, needs and abilities. For this reason, I won't be extolling the virtues of any one particular system. Instead, we will look at the most popular systems around to see what their benefits are and what their disadvantages are. This way, you will have the knowledge necessary to choose the type that is right for you.

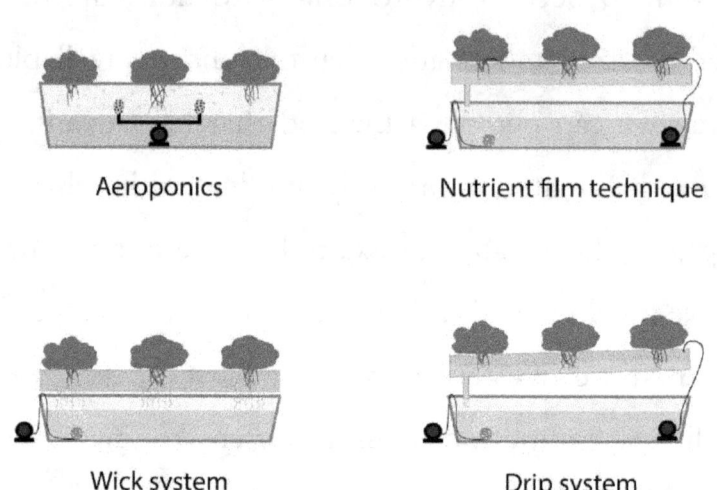

Hydroponic system

Aeroponics

Nutrient film technique

Wick system

Drip system

Drip System

This system is one of the most popular hydroponic setups but it was actually invented for outdoor gardens in Israel. At its most simplified, the drip system uses a pump to keep a drip of nutrient-rich water feeding our plants. The slow drip, rather than the typical spraying of water we see in gardens, allows for less water to be used.

Typically, a drip system is designed with two key parts. The first is the reservoir of nutrient-rich water that will feed the plants. Above this rests the grow tray in which our plants are potted. A pump is set up in the water and is connected up into the grow tray. From there, each of the plants will be given their own drip line. This means if you are growing four plants in your tray, you would use four drip lines. Sixteen plants, sixteen drip lines. The growing medium will slowly release the water back down into the reservoir, creating a closed system.

A drip system offers us great control over the amount of water and nutrients that our plants are getting. With this system we are able to control the drip both by quantity and by length. This means if we use too much water in our drip, we can dial it back; or, if our drip is going too long or too short, we can adjust the timers that we are using to experiment until we find the length that's just right. One of the cool things about the drip system is that while it may take a while to set up and get right in the early period, once we have everything in place and know our volumes, the system doesn't require as much overall maintenance (depending on the particular setup) as other methods will. Plus, the materials needed to create a drip system aren't as costly as some of the others.

Chapter 1. What is Hydroponics?

Hydroponics is a subset of hydroculture, which is a strategy for developing plants without soil by rather utilizing mineral supplement arrangements in water dissolvable. Earthly plants might be developed with just their underlying foundations presented to the nutritious fluid, or the roots might be physically upheld by an idle medium, for example, perlite or rock.

The supplements utilized in hydroponic frameworks can emerge out of a variety of various sources, including (yet not restricted to) from fish stool, duck compost, or bought substance manures.

Plants regularly developed hydroponically include tomatoes, peppers, cucumbers, lettuces.

Plants develop through a procedure called photosynthesis, in which they use daylight and a concoction inside their leaves called chlorophyll to change over carbon dioxide and water into glucose (a kind of sugar) and oxygen. Work that out synthetically and you get this condition:

$$6CO_2 + 6H_2O \rightarrow C_6H_{12}O_6 + 6O_2$$

There's no notice of "soil" anyplace in there—and that is all the verification you need that plants can develop without it. What they do need is water and supplements, both effectively got from soil. Be that as it may, on the off chance that they can get these things elsewhere—by remaining with their underlying foundations in a supplement rich arrangement—they can manage without soil by and large. That is the essential guideline behind hydroponics. In principle, "hydroponics" signifies developing plants in water (from two Greek words signifying "water" and "work"), but since you can develop plants without really standing them in water, a great many people characterize the word to mean developing plants without utilizing soil.

Why Develop Things Hydroponically?

Despite the fact that the advantages of hydroponics have once in a while been addressed, there appear to be numerous points of interest in developing without soil. Some hydroponic producers have discovered they get yields commonly more prominent when they change from customary techniques. Since hydroponically developed plants dunk their foundations legitimately into supplement rich arrangements, they get what they need considerably more effectively than plants developing in soil, so they need a lot smaller root frameworks and can redirect more vitality into leaf and stem development. With smaller roots, you can develop more plants in a similar zone and get more yield from a similar measure of ground (which is especially uplifting news in case you're developing in a restricted region like a nursery or on a gallery or window sill inside). Hydroponic plants additionally come to fruition quicker. Numerous irritations are conveyed in soil, so managing without it by and large gives you a progressively sterile developing framework with less issues of illness. Since hydroponics is perfect for indoor developing, you can utilize it to develop plants lasting through the year. Robotized frameworks constrained by clocks and PCs make the entire thing a breeze.

It's not all uplifting news; unavoidably there are a couple of disadvantages. One is the expense of all the hardware you need—compartments, siphons, lights, supplements, etc. Another downside is the "ponic" portion of hydroponics: there's a sure measure of work included. With customary developing, you can now and again be very high handed about how you treat plants and, if climate and different conditions are your ally, your plants will even now flourish. However, hydroponics is progressively logical and the plants are substantially more heavily influenced by you. You have to check them continually to ensure they're developing in precisely the conditions they need (however robotized frameworks, for example, lighting clocks, make things significantly simpler). Another distinction (seemingly to a lesser extent a downside) is that, in light of the fact that hydroponic plants have a lot smaller root frameworks, they can't generally bolster themselves well overall. Substantial fruiting plants may require very intricate types of help.

Chapter 2. Advantages and Disadvantages

In order for everything to be calm at the home hydro farm, you need to know what advantages and disadvantages of different types of hydroponic systems have. The secret to the success of any undertaking is in choosing the right tools. It is unlikely that you can hammer a nail with the help of a banana. In progressive gardening, such a rule is present everywhere, including when choosing the type of hydroponic system. Each system has its pros and cons, which are worth paying attention to, so as not to fall into frustration.

Wick System

The wick is lowered into a nutrient solution, which rises up under the action of physical laws. The so-called passive system works wonders in the context of the relevance of the motto "cheap, but it works."

Pros:

- Availability. I took a container, poured a substrate - you can plant plants. Hydroponics for dummies;

- Minimum cash costs for maintenance. There is no technology - there are no problems with sensors, programs, and complex systems for providing plants with necessary substances. We need only the initiative of a cheerful water-carrier freedman;

- Without a feed pump. Since physics is the main driving force of the process, then additional assistance for the supply of nutrients to the roots of plants is not necessary.

Disadvantages:

- Limited access to oxygen to water or solution. It can cause a whole bunch of problems - stale water, problems with the root system, and so on.

- Slow growth. An independent plant cannot fully grow in breadth and height as a beginner would like if he had seen enough of the giant strawberry bushes on other hydroponic farms;

- No nutrient recycling. And why? That's right; because there is no pump. There is nothing to add.

Deepwater Crop System (DWC)

Higher than passive systems, but not having all the charms of hi-tech and engineering peaks, choice. A simple device, but with a "whistle" - a compressor that delivers oxygen to the nutrient solution, nourishing the root system. Which, in turn, is located in a mesh pot and installed in the lid of the tank with a nutrient solution.

Pros:

- The cheapest option from active systems. Savings - a necessity in a precarious American economy;
- Ease of setup and reliability. Based on the foregoing, an undeniable plus for advanced beginners;
- Without a feed pump. The same plus as in the wick system;
- Reliable, due to the small number of brittle elements;

- A decent supply of solution guarantees the safety of your plants;

- Everything is growing and fast.

Disadvantages:

- Risk of root rot with insufficiently regular cleaning.

- With a high level of solution and excessive over moistening, the likelihood of decay of the root neck is high;

- The need to constantly replenish the tank. A regular run for water and nutritious mixtures is a good help for losing weight, but not for progressive crop production.

Periodic Flooding System

A method that is also striking in its simplicity. Plants can be placed on top of each other, and the liquid flowing from one pot gets into another. Simple and tasteful. Of course, you can make an advanced option, with valves and sensors, which will allow you to control the liquid level in the substrate, which is good for the hydroponics and his wards.

Pros:

- Availability. In order to make an average hydroponic installation, you do not need to order tons of equipment and spend a lot of time choosing a manufacturer and understand a billion nuances;

- Low costs. The simplicity of the technology entails a small amount of money for maintenance;

- Good saturation with a nutrient solution. Nutrients pass through the entire substrate. Vigorous growth and high productivity available.

Disadvantages:

- Like any reversible system, there is a risk of contamination of the solution with pathogens'

- The risk of mold and other "water" weeds. If there is a lot of water, then parasites will certainly appear, which will live there freely;

- Technical malfunctions can lead to a decrease in yield. If any valves get stuck, or the water separation system itself is de-energized, then goodbye to normal watering, and as a result, caput to the mountains of vegetables.

Drip Irrigation System

This is hydroponics "as it is." A description is not required, however, this system has its advantages and disadvantages. First of all, it is worth noting that drip irrigation does not require special intervention in the process by humans. But it is worth decently investing in so that everything works like a clock.

Pros:

- The nutrient solution goes to "5+ stars". The system is so good that it is used by most hydroponic firms in the West;

- A sufficient supply of oxygen to the root system. This means that there should not be any problems with the circulation of nutrients. Consequently, the seedlings will grow and turn into the pride of a gardener, just as per the instructions.

Disadvantages:

- The biggest minus is the need for regular cleaning to eliminate blockages in the irrigation system. And a similar method is fraught with the development of mold on the roots and containers.

Aeroponics

"Ferrari" hydroponics. The most effective method for growing vegetables, fruits, and other flora on an industrial scale. But for a home farm, it suits well enough, although you have to sweat in order to understand all the intricacies of technology. Although the profit from this is rather big.

Pros:

- Maximum absorption of nutrients. Due to aeroponic technology, as many substances as the plant needs come to the roots;

- Efficient use of space. You can arrange the trays at least in three layers, the "kids" will only be a joy. There will be no empty space for sure. So, the harvest will be such that before spring is enough.

Disadvantages:

- Blockages, blockages, and again blockages. Nowhere to go from them. Therefore, you need to regularly check all nodes, contacts, and sensors. You can say goodbye to personal life and cheating;

- Aeroponics is poorly suited for thick nutrient mixtures. This cannot be called a drawback, but for the ignorant, it can serve as a motivation to throw crop production into the far corner along with cross-stitch and modeling.

Choosing the Right Hydroponic System

Be that as it may, hydroponics requires a thorough study of the theoretical part. Well, the choice of a hydroponic system depends entirely on personal preferences, your scale of operation, and the cost you are willing to spare in your hydroponic operation.

Chapter 3.   Equipment's

Monitoring Equipment

pH meter

pH is a measure of how acidic or how alkaline water is. A pH of 7 is neutral. pH levels that range from 1 to 6 are acidic, and levels from 8 to 14 are considered alkaline or basic.

Different plants have their preferences regarding pH levels. To ensure the best possible growth, you need to have a way of testing and then adjusting the pH level of your water.

For example:

- Cabbage likes pH levels of 7.5
- Tomatoes like a pH of 6-6.5
- Sweet potatoes like a pH of 5.2-6
- Peppers like a pH of 5.5-7
- Lettuce and broccoli like a pH of 6-7

We will talk about why balancing pH is essential later in the book.

A pH meter can be obtained from local hydroponics stores or online. You need to calibrate the sensor with the calibration powder that comes with the meter. A basic pH meter will cost you $10 to $20.

A basic pH meter

Don't use paper test strips for the water because they are inaccurate. Most of the time, a pH meter is offered in combination with a TDS or EC meter, which we will talk about next.

EC meter

Electrical conductivity is a measurement of how easily electricity passes through the water, the higher the ion content, the better it is at conducting electricity.

All water has ions in it. When you add nutrients to the water, you are increasing the ion content, effectively increasing the electrical conductivity.

EC or Electrical Conductivity is an integral part of the hydroponics equation. The simplest way of explaining this is as a guide to salts dissolved in water. Its unit is Siemens per meter, but in hydroponics, we use millisiemens per meter.

In short, the higher the number of salts in the water, the higher the conductivity. Water that has no salt (distilled water) will have zero conductivity.

Lettuce likes an EC of 1.2 (or 1.2 millisiemens), while basil likes an EC of 2.

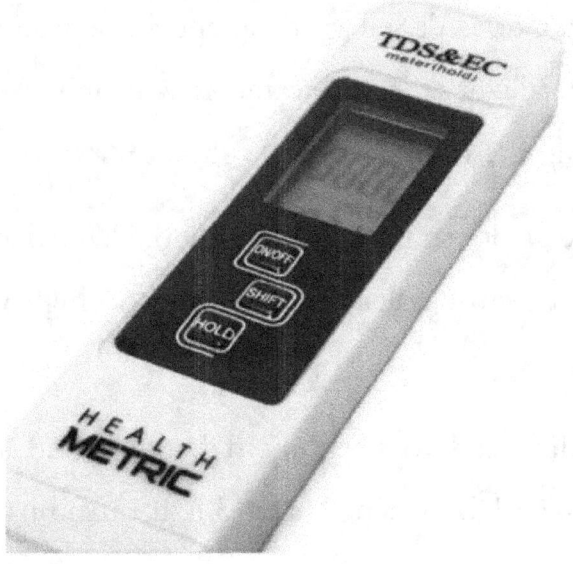

A $15 TDS & EC meter from amazon

That is why it is so important to know your EC and what your plants prefer, it will help you to ensure your system is at the right level.

However, electrical conductivity needs are also affected by the weather. When it is hot, the plants evaporate more water. That is why you need to decrease the EC in hot summer months. In colder winter months, you need to increase the EC.

- In warm weather, you need to decrease the EC.

- In cold weather, you need to increase the EC.

An EC meter doesn't tell you the specific amount of which mineral or fertilizer is in the water. If you only use a nutrient solution using the right ratios, you shouldn't worry.

Just because it doesn't monitor individual nutrients, doesn't mean it's not useful. Salt levels that are too high will damage your plants.

You generally need to keep them between 0.8 and 1.2 for leafy greens and between 2 and 3.5 for fruiting crops like tomatoes. The source of the water can influence the EC reading. More on this later.

Sometimes, you see the recommended nutrient levels listed as CF. CF is the conductivity factor. This is like EC, used in Europe. If you multiply EC by ten, you will become CF.

For example, lettuce grows best in an EC of 0.8 to 1.2. This is a CF of 8 to 12.

TDS meter

TDS stands for total dissolved salts. You may hear some hydroponics growers referring to the TDS and not EC. These are both used to determine the strength of your hydroponic solution. If you buy a TDS meter, there will also be an option to switch to EC readings.

TDS readings are converted from an EC reading. The problem occurs when you don't know which calculation method was used to produce the TDS; there are several different ones.

In general, EC and CF readings are used in Europe, while TDS is an American measurement. But, regardless of which measurement you choose to use, they are both effectively the same thing: a measure of the nutrient levels in your solution.

The NaCl Conversion factor

This is effectively measuring salt in the water. You'll find most TDS meters use 0.5. This is the easiest one for you to remember and calculate. Most of the meters sold will use the NaCl conversion factor.

As an example, if you have a reading of 1 EC (1 milli Siemens or 1000 micro Siemens), you will have a TDS reading of

500ppm.

1000 micro Siemens x 0.5 = 500ppm

Natural Water Conversion factor

This conversion factor is referred to as the 4-4-2; this quantifies its contents. Forty percent sodium sulfate, forty percent sodium bicarbonate, and twenty percent sodium chloride.

Again, the conversion factor is a range, this time between 0.65 and 0.85. Most TDS meters will use 0.7.

For example, 1 EC (1000 micro Siemens) will be 700 ppm with a TDS meter that uses the natural water conversion.

1000 micro Siemens x 0.7 = 700ppm

Potassium Chloride, KCl Conversion factor

1000 micro Siemens x 0.55 = 550ppm

These are not all the possible conversion options, but they are the most common. The first, NaCl is the most used today.

Dissolved oxygen sensor

Plant roots need oxygen to remain healthy and ensure the plant grows properly. The dissolved oxygen sensor will help you to understand how much oxygen is available in the water and ensure it's enough to keep your plants healthy.

If plants don't get enough oxygen to their roots, they can die. A minimum of 5 ppm is recommended.

A dissolved oxygen meter will be expensive for the hobbyist to buy, especially when you are starting. That is why dissolved oxygen meters are generally not purchased by people who do hydroponics for fun. A good meter can cost you $170 to $500 for a reputable brand.

You do not need to invest in one if you oxygenate the water. Oxygenation of the water can be done by using an air pump with an air stone in the water tank. Depending on the method of growing, you don't need to aerate the water.

The dissolved oxygen in the water will be at its lowest during the summer. The water heats up, and the dissolved oxygen becomes less available. While your plants can do very well in winter, they might lack oxygen during summer.

Net Pots

In some systems, you are going to need net pots to hold the plants. This is mostly true for deep water culture (DWC), Kratky, wick systems, Aeroponics, fogponics, Dutch buckets, and possibly vertical towers.

Make sure you get the net pots with a lip on top to keep them from falling through. The standard size for lettuce is two inches (five centimeters). If you want to use tomatoes with Dutch buckets, six inches (fifteen centimeters) is recommended.

3 and 2-inch (7 and 5 cm) net pots

If you are creating a new system on a budget, there are a variety of other options that can be used instead of buying net pots. For example, plastic cups with lots of holes in them, or simply fine netting on a wireframe. Use your imagination!

6-inch (15 cm) net pots for a 5-gallon (18 liters) bucket

Humidity And Temperature Sensor

Estimating temperatures and humidity levels will lead to mistakes. I recommend getting a simple humidity and temperature sensor, so you don't need to guess. Most of them will cost you no more than $15.

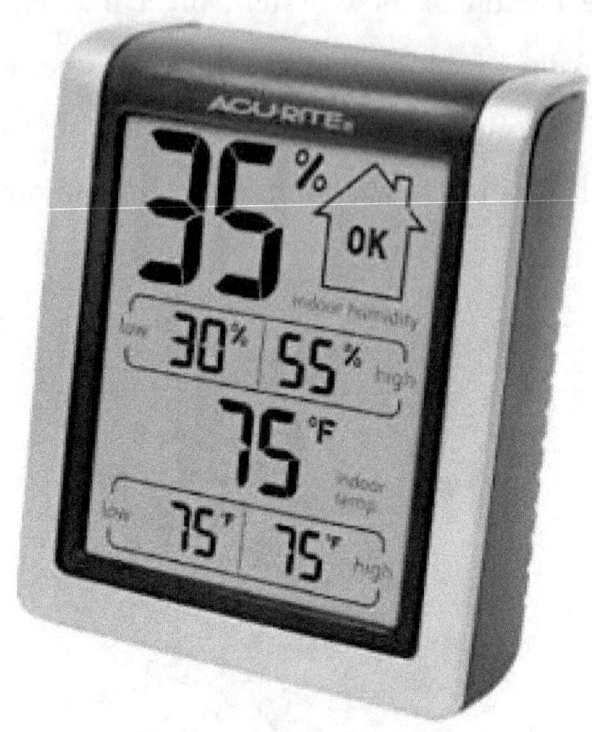

Accurate humidity and temperature sensor

Germination Tray And Dome

You need to start seeds in a dedicated germination tray. Most of these trays are 10x10 or 10x20 inches (25x25 or 25x50 centimeters) and generally include a humidity dome.

These trays are used to let your seeds germinate and keep the humidity high. After the first true leaves appear, it is time to transplant them into your system. Usually, this is after ten to fifteen days.

The humidity should be between sixty and seventy percent, while temperatures should be 68-77°F or 20-25°C.

A 10x10 germination tray with humidity dome

Seed Starter Cubes

If you are growing plants from seed, you can't simply place seeds in the net pots. They'll get washed away or sink. Instead, you need a seed starter cube. These cubes provide a place for the seed to start growing roots and flourish, safely.

Several materials can be used as your grow media when starting seeds:

Rockwool cubes

These are made from a combination of basalt and chalk, spun together. The result is a small cube that is similar in consistency to cotton candy. Your seeds can be placed into the Rockwool cube where they will start to germinate. The cube goes in the net pot and your seed should have everything it needs to start growing. Providing it has access to the nutrient-rich water. These cubes come in all shapes and sizes.

Groan 1-inch (2.5cm) Rockwool cubes

Generally, you would only need a small one or one and a half inch or cube. Depending on the method of growing, you need to add some grow media to support the cube and block sunlight from creating algae on the cube.

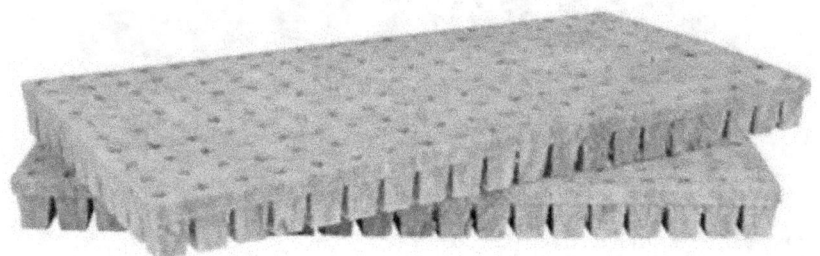

Two seed starting cubes sheets

You can separate each cube from the bigger sheet. I recommend using gloves for this because the Rockwool can be irritating on the skin.

As with every seed starter cube, you must soak it in pH neutral water of six before using it. This ensures that the seed has better germination rates.

Coco Coir

An alternative to Rockwool cubes is coco coir. This is simply the fibrous coat of a coconut.

Coco coir is sold in briquettes

Coco coir is an organic media which will break down over time. Some people use it because it is environmentally friendly and renewable. I don't recommend it to start with. It can break down and clog your system if you are not careful. It can begin to rot somewhere, and before you know it, make your water quality terrible.

Oasis cubes

Another seed-starting cube is the oasis cube. They retain moisture well and are very soft. This makes it easy for the roots to penetrate the medium but also makes them brittle. Oasis cubes are also used as a growing media. These cubes are very popular with NFT systems.

Oasis starter cubes

Sponges

Sponges are used most of the time as a cheap alternative to Rockwool or oasis cubes. However, they do not absorb or retain moisture that well. That is why using sponges is not a carefree method of seed starting. They are not as environmentally friendly as the other seed starting cubes.

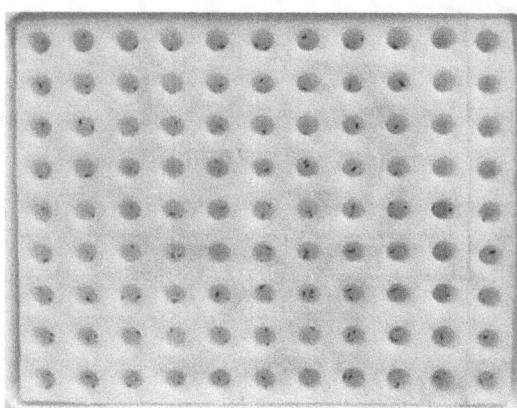

Seed starting sponges

Growing media

After you have placed your seed in the seed starter cubes and they have started to germinate, you will see roots coming out of the starter cube.

This is the time for you to start transplanting them into their second grow space. The grow media will depend on which growing technique you are going to use.

For floating rafts and NFT, you do not need any growing media. For other methods like the Kratky, Dutch buckets, or wick system, you may need to add some growing media.

The use of grow media also depends on how big the plant is going to be. Lettuce doesn't need growing media because it doesn't need the support. Tomatoes need growing media to support the plant.

Growing media gives your plant stability and space for the roots to further develop.

Hydro ton

This is the most popular growing media.

Hydro ton is created from clay that has been heated to high temperatures. The result is a very porous material that is made into small balls.

Hydro ton is very lightweight, ensuring your pots aren't under any undue stress. It is excellent to keep your seed starter cubes in place. It's also easy on the hands.

Hydro ton

You should wash hydro ton before using it to remove clay dust.

You can also re-sterilize this grow media, but it can be time-consuming, especially if you have a lot of it.

Sterilizing or re-sterilizing is vital as your grow media can have bacteria or other micro-organisms that could be harmful to your plants. Whether using it for the first time or re-using the growing media, cleaning alone may not be enough to get rid of these bacteria. You need to sterilize the growing media to ensure it is safe for re-use.

Sterilizing involves using either heat or a chemical to kill all organisms on the growing media. A popular chemical choice is hydrogen peroxide.

You will need a thirty-five percent hydrogen peroxide solution and then wash the clay balls in it thoroughly. Mix one part of hydrogen peroxide (thirty-five percent) with eleven parts of water. This will lower it to a three percent solution.

Most importantly, you need to rinse the growing media several times to ensure all traces of the hydrogen peroxide are gone.

You could also use a ten percent bleach solution. A bleach solution is used for sterilizing NFT troughs or other equipment in your system as well.

The alternative is to heat the growing media in an oven with a temperature of 180°F (82°C) or more, for at least thirty minutes. It will pasteurize and remove fungal type microorganisms. To get rid of all organisms, you need to sterilize which involves at least thirty minutes at 212°F (100°C).

Warning: Doing this in your kitchen will leave a sour odor that lingers.

A Rockwool seed-starter cube placed in hydro ton grow media

Perlite

When you take minerals and expose them to extreme heat,

you will force them to expand and pop like popcorn, effectively creating Perlite. This is another growing media that is pH neutral and extremely light. It's not good at retaining moisture.

Perlite as a growing media

Perlite is used by gardeners in their soil to increase aeration to the roots. It is excellent for Dutch buckets (drip), wicking systems, or the Kratky method. More on these later.

You can get Perlite at any garden store, but you must be

careful not to get it in your eyes.

When handling perlite, use a dust mask. The dust created when handling perlite is not healthy to breathe in.

Vermiculite

Vermiculite growing media

This silicon-based substance is exposed to the same high temperatures for forming Perlite. It also expands and is very similar to Perlite, and it is also pH neutral. The main difference is that Vermiculite is high in cation-exchange.

In simple terms, it is better at holding onto water and

nutrition for release into the plant later. Vermiculite is too good at retaining moisture that it can suffocate the roots. That's why it's popular in a fifty/fifty mix with perlite.

Rockwool

As already described, Rockwool is an excellent choice for seed starting. The larger Rockwool cubes that range from three to six inches (seven to fifteen centimeters) can be used for an entire plant. It is pH neutral and easy to use. Rockwool is very good at wicking up the water.

Big Rockwool cubes

The big Rockwool cubes are mostly used for plants that have a long-life cycle. It is not financially viable to plant lettuce in these bigger grow blocks. The holes in these blocks are too big for seedlings. You need to use a Rockwool starter cube to grow your seedlings, and then move the plant with the starter cube into these bigger cubes.

Another method of growing is using Rockwool slabs. They are widely used in tomato farms. They are the largest Rockwool media you can find. You can fit several big rock wool cubes in one slab. One slab is a few feet long and comes in different sizes. You need to pre-soak these too.

Seed starting cubes fitted into big Rockwool cubes, fitted into a Rockwool grow slab.

Do not remove the plastic cover from these. The plastic keeps the moisture in and the light out. Drainage holes should be made at the bottom of the slab. Drip emitters should be inserted into the big Rockwool cubes.

Grow stones

Grow stones are made from recycled glass, which may seem like an unusual material for a hydroponics system.

Grow stones

Grow stones are good for aeration and moisture retention. The fact that they can wick water up to four inches (ten centimeters) above the waterline means your plants will always have the water they need.

You shouldn't let the term glass put you off, they look like sharp edges, but they are not.

River rock

As the name suggests, this type of grow material comes from a riverbed. The rocks are naturally rounded off as the water removes the sharp edges. The irregular shapes of river rock means that there are plenty of air pockets, which makes it easier for the roots to become established.

If you are operating a flood and drain style hydroponics system, this can be the right choice. But, if you need more water retention, river rock might not be the best option out there.

If you are on a tight budget and hydro ton is a bit too expensive, river rock will be the best alternative. Use three-quarter inch (two centimeters) river rock for the best results.

¾ inch (2 cm) river rock

River rock must be washed before you use it to ensure it is clean. If you are thinking of using this, it is worth noting that it is cumbersome, potentially preventing you from moving your system in the future.

Chapter 4. Lighting and Heat

When building and equipping an efficient hydroponics greenhouse capable of producing crops throughout the year, the producer should consider the aspects that we show below. These ten recommendations, from the owner of successful hydroponic operation in Florida, United States, could help you plan or improve your operation.

1. Place and orientation of the structure, towards true north.

Exposure to the sun throughout the day (east and west) may provide too much heat during the summer, but it will increase the hours of light and warmth when you really need it during the winter, the season in which crops tend to grow more slowly. It is more profitable to cool the greenhouse in the summer than to have to provide the necessary light to perform photosynthesis and adequate heat in the growing season.

2. Firm, tight, and solid structure.

If you want to produce the 12 months of the year successfully, it is essential to start with a firm, hermetic, and well-built structure. If you limit yourself to using tubular frames and double polyethylene sheath, you will only produce seasonal crops, or you will fail in the attempt to produce throughout the year.

3. Concrete foundations, with mooring beams and support walls.

If you want to install air conditioning in summer, you must seal the structure from the base to the ridge. Do not take shortcuts in the construction of a suitable structure. If you take a shortcut, you will eventually lose out, since you will not be able to compensate for the heat gain.

4. High-quality polycarbonate covers.

New polycarbonate covers are available in the market. Select the material of the appropriate quality according to your crops, the performance of the material in the long term, and the transmission of the required light. Avoid cheap and low-quality covers, or you'll end up paying three times more by having to replace those series times during the life of the structure. In horticulture, you only get what you pay for, therefore use only the best.

5. Shade mesh suitable for heat fighting.

First, never use black shadow mesh to cope with heat gain. Only a suitable shade grade mesh can reflect the heat of the ship. If you use black mesh on or under the surface, the only thing you will get is more significant heat gain, and the structural steel will retain this heat, which you will have to mitigate throughout the day.

6. Water for cooling the air mass.

You can use the end wall of the structure to lower the temperature. Many producers are concerned about the size of the wet wall surface, as they think more is better; But this is not so. To calculate the degree of cooling of a ship, first, you have to estimate the volume of it in cubic meters, and then calculate the amount of air or cooling you need for each degree you want to reduce.

The ship must be completely sealed so that there are no openings or air inlets, even around the doors. Once the building is appropriately sealed, consider the volume of air. If you need to move between 1,700 and 2,800 cubic meters of air, the air inlet-outlet ratio should be 1: 1. To achieve this, you have to calculate your fans or fans so that they move the air throughout the given space minute. This is not easily achieved, since you need fans of high volume, from 130 to 150 cm, similar to those used in dairies. These fans are expensive, and it is necessary that the end walls are welded with heavy steel to support them. Keep in mind that the force of moving so much air through the ship is comparable to a series of wind blows against the building for 18 to 20 hours a day. If the ship is like 95% of the greenhouses in the market, the structure will be destroyed.

7. Volume and water storage.

If you want to cool the interior of the ship to a temperature between 22 and 30 ° C, the industry-standard wet wall will not be enough, since high volumes of water are required, almost like a small waterfall. It is necessary to have a minimum reservoir of 2,000 liters, but it is recommended to have 3,800 liters due to high evaporation losses. The best pumps are those of & frac34; at 1 CV of power in total flow volume. The wet wall panels will have to be built to order and make sure they are plumb. When the amount of the air mass is passed through the wet wall panels, the temperature drops, and high evaporation occurs. As the accelerated air passes through the structure, it extracts heat from a particular area and directs it towards the fans. Avoid low airflow or around the cooling panels. Make sure the air is directed to and through the water column.

8. Cost according to the expected profit.

In the month of August, if you require a 500 square meter ship to be cool during the day and the cold at night, you will spend between $ 5,500 and 6,500 pesos per square meter. If you have a crop of high demand throughout the year, you can recover the cost by lengthening the growing season, but make sure you have a plan and a market for your crops.

9. The temperature of nutrients is essential to avoid diseases.

The temperature of the nutrients is as important as the cooling air to cool the plants under a hydroponic system. This is essential to avoid pathogen problems and diseases. You can't wait for the air to do everything for you. Most producers use commercial heat exchangers to cool the nutrient solution. This is another quite expensive area and has to be precisely sized to fit your structure and your crops. Mathematics will be your new ally, so get a good calculator and a banker.

10. Maintenance and cleaning are vital.

Keep your structure extremely clean and weeds very far from the ships. A minimum surface area of 15 meters around the buildings and 30 meters behind the wet wall should be kept impeccable if possible. Use a 50-mesh mesh to keep pest pressure down. Build vestibules or hallways so that when you open a door, all the air from the wet wall is pulled into the zone of minimum resistance. This pressure sucks and attracts any object (from small birds to an employee's wig) to the fans in a matter of seconds, and is particularly useful with greenhouse insects.

Natural Lights

One of the most important things you need to learn about when you are learning about growing with hydroponics, besides the actual system, is the lighting.

If your plants do not receive the light they need, they are not going to grow properly nor are they going to produce the amount of fruit you want. To become the best grower, you always want to find out what is limiting you the most. Learning what is limiting you the most and learning as much about it as you can is going to allow you to increase the growth of your plants without adjusting anything else.

When you think about lighting, you have to realize that no matter how great your system is, no matter how great the medium you are using is, no matter how high the quality of your fertilizer, without the proper light, your plants will never be able to grow healthy, strong plants.

The first thing you have to know about is the color of light that your bulbs produce. You see, every bulb will produce a colored light that is measured in degrees Kelvin; this is how the hue produced by the bulb is specified.

Most plants are going to grow better with a bulb that is 6500° degrees Kelvin. Flowering plants, on the other hand, are going to grow better at 2700k degrees Kelvin.

Of course, there are many different variables that will affect the rate at which your plants grow, but the most important of these variables is light. Using a high quality light is the only way you can guarantee your plants will grow to their fullest potential.

Artificial Lights

There are a number of lighting systems on the market today and each of these systems have their own pro's and con's that need to be taken into consideration, but it is important for you to remember that choosing the correct lighting for your indoor growing is the most important thing you can do to ensure effective growing.

Incandescent lamps are the first of the lighting systems that I want to talk about. These are what are known as the standard household light bulbs, and they are not very efficient when it comes to growing plants. They actually only have about a 5% efficiency rate. Incandescent lamps are not recommended for growing plants.

Fluorescent lights are a great choice if you are planning on growing your plants indoors. The best fluorescent lights are high output lights, which are about 7 times more efficient. This simply means that the lights will put out more light while using less electricity. A wide range of spectrums are available when it comes to fluorescent lamps and the 6500k are the best for indoor growing.

If you are growing larger plants, using fluorescent lighting is not advised as these are better for smaller plants. The fluorescent lamps are not as good at penetrating as the high intensity discharge lamps are.

There are many options for growing plants when it comes to fluorescent lights. You can choose lights that will be hung above the plants or that are hung to the side of the plants.

Another very popular form of fluorescent lights are the compact fluorescent lights or CFLs. These were designed as an alternative to the normal household bulbs or incandescent lights because they use less electricity and are supposed to have a longer life than incandescent bulbs. The CFL's are good for growers who are on a small budget and are growing small plants.

The great thing about CFLs is that you do not have to worry about the wiring, they don't require anything more than a standard socket, and they are extremely low in price. If you are going to use CFLs, you should consider using a reflector of some type, otherwise you will be wasting a lot of light that you could be using for your plants.

High intensity discharge lamps are the next type of lighting that I want to talk to you about. Also known as HID, these bulbs are the top pick for most growers. These are usually the types are generally used in street lights, parking lots, and warehouses. These lights are the top pick for today's growers because their output is 8 times more efficient than regular household light bulbs.

Light emitting diodes or LEDs are some of the new technology that growers are using for their plants because they use much less electricity than the other light sources mentioned.

There are many different things you need to think about when you are choosing your lighting. Your budget is the first thing that you need to think about when you are choosing your lighting for your hydroponics system. Those who are working with a low budget will be better off using T5 fluorescent tubes as will small scale growers.

If you have a large budget, the HID lamps are the highest quality, but you will need to consider getting them their own ventilation system because they will significantly raise the temperature of the room otherwise.

LED lights are great for those who are going to be growing for a long period of time because they will save you a ton of money on your electric bill. For example, some growers save as much as $5,000 over the lifetime of their LED bulbs.

Of course, this is just an example and it all depends on the price of electricity, how much you are willing to invest upfront, how often you use the lights, the type of environment the lighting system will be in, and so forth.

Once you have chosen your hydroponics system and your medium, you will need to spend some time thinking about the type of lighting system you will be using. It is important to remember that the lighting system is the most important factor when it comes to growing your plants indoors and it is not something you should take lightly.

Chapter 5.   Hydroponics Grow System

It will walk you through all of the materials that you need for each system, as well as walk you through setting it up. You can build it from these instructions or build it on a larger scale. It will depend on the needs of what plants you want to grow.

Wick Hydroponic System

This system is one of the easiest systems of all six; due to it not needing any moving parts. Therefore, you will not need a pump or any electricity to power the system. However, some individuals like to use an air pump inside the reservoir.

Materials

- 2 Buckets (1 for the plant/1 for the reservoir)
- Wick growing media. (Coco Coir, Perlite, or Vermiculite)
- Strips of material (felt) or wick rope.

The way this system operates is by using a wick. It soaks up the solution and provides it to the roots of the plant. It sucks up the nutrient solution that is located in the reservoir using the process of capillary action. Normally the wick system will have two or more sized wicks that will supply the water to the plant. The bucket with the plant will sit on top of the reservoir bucket.

Wicks

The wick is the most important part of this system because without it the nutrient solution will not be given to your plants, and in result the plants will die to lack of moisture and nutrition. If you are unsure of what to use, then you will need to do a little bit of experimenting to ensure that you are offering your plants enough solution. You need to use something that is absorbent, yet is still resistant to the rotting process. Make sure that you wash the wick very well before you use it. It will significantly improve its ability of most materials that are used.

Some of the most common materials that people use for wicks are things like:

- Propylene Felt Strips
- Fibrous Rope
- Rayon Rope

- Tiki Torch Wicks
- Braided Polyurethane Yarn
- Wool Rope
- Wool Felt
- Nylon Rope
- Cotton Rope
- Old Clothes
- Old Blankets

Ensure that there are enough wicks in order to support the water usage of the plant roots. This will depend on how you are building your system, type of plant that you are growing, and what medium you are using. You will need at least 2-4 wicks unless the system is extremely small. Another important note is that the less the wick has to travel to provide the solution, the more water it can offer the roots.

Once the solution makes it up through the wick into the growing media, you need to use an absorbent media to hold the moisture. Some of the most typically used media's for wick systems are Vermiculite, coco coir, or even perlite. In some cases, even polymer crystals can be used.

Reservoir

The reservoir can be large or even small; you just do not want it to run dry fast. Also you will want the water levels to be high enough so that the water does not need to travel up too far to get to the growing media or the root zone. You will want to top off your reservoir with fresh solution as it is needed, as well as clean it and change it completely every so often as well. You do not want algae or microorganisms to grow in the water. Due to the wick sucking up the solution evenly, the plants do not use or absorb more than necessary.

Directions

- Step 1: Cotton rope is one of the easiest wicks to use; however, it is subject to rotting, so try to use nylon rope instead. Test the wick's ability, washed, as well as unwashed.
- Step 2: Mix up the solution in the bucket and punch a hole in the top of the lid. Thread your wick through the hole. Snap the lid on the bucket.
- Step 3: Cut down 5-gallon pots and force it on the inside so that the media will not wash out of the holes. Thread the wick through the bottom of the pot and spread them out on the bottom.

- Step 4: Put about an inch of the media in the bottom of the pot for the plant to grow. Fill the rest of the container with about 50/50 perlite/vermiculite. Pre-moisten your media. Sprinkle your seeds, and then set it in the sun.

Water Culture Systems

The water culture system is also one of the easiest systems of the basic hydroponics systems. They are still extremely effective for growing different types of plants. Not only do most home hydroponic growers like this type of system, but many of the commercial growers also use this system on a grander scale. It is because the water culture method is easy and typically inexpensive. It is also great for those who want to use a hydroponic system at home. Even though this system is easy to build, there are many different variations and different materials that are used to carry out this system.

Materials

- Storage Tote
- Air Pump (30-60 Gallon Aquarium)
- Air Line
- Air Stones

- 8 – 3 Inch Net Baskets for Each Plant
- Growing Media
- Black Spray Paint
- White Spray Paint

How this system works is pretty easy. The plant is suspended in the baskets above the solution inside the reservoir. Typically by Styrofoam that is floating on the top or even through holes that are cut in the lid that is on the reservoir. The roots then hang down from the containers that the plant is in, and they hang down into the solution where they are submerged with the solution. The plant roots stay submerged at all times. The plant roots do not suffocate due to getting air and oxygen from the bubbles rising from the pump in the solution.

The more bubbles in the solution, the better. The bubbles rise through the solution and make the water look like it is boiling. Bubbles should be coming up through and making contact with the plant roots as they rise to the top of the solution. There are two ways of offering aeration and dissolved oxygen to the solution.

Aeration Types

- Bubbles: Typically an aquarium pump and air stones are used to offer bubbles to the solution in the water for this type of system, as well as other methods of hydroponics. The pump offers air volume and it is connected to the stones with an air tube. The stones are made from porous rock or other types of similar material. It has small pores that will create small bubbles that will rise to the top of the solution. Soaker hose can also be used in the place of the stones to create the bubbles. The soaker hose offers smaller bubbles. The smaller bubbles will better aerate the solution. Smaller bubbles offer more contact to the surface of the water. Contact between the bubbles and water will help to replace the dissolved oxygen that is taken by the plant roots.
- Falling Water: Most home hydroponics will not face the problem of surface agitation; however, there are some that will need the agitation. The higher the water is from the falling point, the more agitation there is on the surface. The more

downward the force, the deeper the agitation is and the more it is aerated. This technique of aeration is typically used in the commercial systems since they use large volume of the solution in comparison to the home hydroponic systems.

Recirculating the System

Another variation of this is the recirculating water culture technique. This variation works almost like a flood and draining system. However, it never really drains. You can have numerous containers connected to the reservoir. Each container has its own fill line and drain tube that will drain back into the reservoir. Some growers use buckets. Each of the buckets has one plant in it and is filled with the solution. There may be a row of buckets. As the solution fills the buckets, the excess solution spills over in the tube and then backs into the reservoir. It is then circulated back into the plants.

Most of those who have this type of system will recirculate the solution like this so that the solution is not wasted and they use a pump in the central reservoir. They allow the water to pump consistently. However, if you have bubbles running in the buckets like a typical water cutler, you can vary the time on for the pump. Also the plants will benefit from the direct contact with the bubbles.

Recirculating the solution will allow you to be able to use the falling water as a source of aerating the solution. You do not need to keep watching the level of the water in each of the containers. Another benefit is when you are growing larger plants; this will ensure they get enough solution.

Directions

- Step 1: Cut 8 spaced holes for the 3-inch net pots in the lid of your tote. Make sure that you do not cut the holes too big; you can always cut the holes bigger if they prove to be too small. But if you cut it too big there is no going back.
- Step 2: Put the lid on the tote facing upwards on newspaper, and then storage tote bottom. Paint both of the pieces black with the paint. Painting them black will keep the light out and keep the algae from growing. Allow it to dry completely.
- Step 3: Paint the pieces that you had painted black with the white paint. This will reflect the sun from the containers so that the solution does not get to

hot or evaporate too quickly.

- Step 4: Cut another smaller hole in the middle of the lid that is large enough for you to run flexible air hose through it. Put your stones inside the grow chamber and then connect the lines to the stones. Run the air lines up through the hole you made in the lid.

- Step 5: Close the lid and then connect the lines to the pump. Do not use the one-way check value that came with the pump, they will clog and then block the air. Instead ensure that you put the air pump at least 6-8 inches above the solution line.

- Step 6: Ensure that the storage totes are completely level that way the solution will also be level inside the chamber.

- Step 7: Put your 3-inch baskets in the holes you cut in the lid. Fill the storage tote with the solution so that the baskets are hanging in it about ½ of an inch.

- Step 8: Fill the pots with the growing media of your choosing. You are able to use any of the media you would like; however, coco chips are highly suggested for this type of system due to it being able to pick up the solution.

Ebb & Flow System

This system is also called a flood and drains system and is the most classic type of setup. It is extremely easy to understand, create, as well as maintain. It is versatile and is able to accommodate pots of many sizes. There are many plants that can be put on the table or the growing bed. Periodically, the solution is pumped into the flooding bed. The plants are watered from the bottom. After a few minutes of the plant roots soaking in the solution, the pump then cuts it off, and then the table drains. The solution returns to the reservoir at the bottom. The cycle will repeat 2-4 times daily. It is simple, yet very effective.

Materials:

- Black Storage Tote (18 gallon)
- Snap toppers Clear Tray (30 quart)
- Timer with 15 Minute Increments
- Aquarium Pump
- 6 Feet of Airline Tube
- T Connector

- 4 Flower Pots (8 inches)
- Bag of Perlite
- Black Irrigation Tubing (1/2 inch – 18 inches long)
- Pond Pump (120 gph)
- Fill and Drain Fitting (set with one extension)
- Brick of Coco Coir
- Small Bag of Clay Balls
- Power Drill

Directions

- Step 1: Cut two 1-¼ inch holes in the middle of the clear tray. Smooth the edges with sandpaper.
- Step 2: Put the clear tray on the top of the black tote lid, and then center it both ways. Mark the center of the hole in the tray in the black lid using a marker.
- Step 3: Cut two more same sized holes in the lid. You will be lining up the holes.
- Step 4: Screw the two fittings into the holes of the clear tote. The rubber gasket will go on the underside of the tote. Tighten it securely. Do not use tools it will strip the fittings. Put only one

extension on the tube for overflow.

- Step 5: Put ½ inch irrigation tubing on the water pump outlet fitting. It will need to be snug. You may have to use a zip tie.

- Step 6: Put the clear tray on the drain fitting and then put it over the black lid. Line u the holes. They need to line up perfecting and the fitting should drop down through the holes that were put in the black lid.

- Step 7: Trim the ½ inch black tubing so that it is the length that will allow the pump to sit on the bottom of the tote that is being used as the reservoir once the lid is on. You will have to try it all out to ensure the measurements are accurate before assembling it to run.

- Step 8: Drop in the bubbler stone to the bottom of the black bin and then rn the airline tube and the pump plug through the port that you drilled. Put the lid and the tray to the tote. Snap them into place.

- Step 9: You will need to make a dipstick. Use a 1 x 1 stick or even a wood dowel. This will help you later to gauge the solution level without having to remove the top and the plants.

- Step 10: Fill the reservoir with 10 gallons of water. Add in the nutrient of your choice. Adjust the pH of your solution using a test kit. Plug up the bubbler and the pump and then test the system to ensure that it is operational and has no leaks.
- Step 11: You will need to drill ¼ inch holes around the sides of the pots in order to provide a good fill and drain mark for the solution.
- Step 12: Fill your pots with the hydroponics medium. It is recommended to use 50/50 mixture of perlite and coco coir with an inch of LECA on the bottom.
- Step 13: Plant the seeds in the pots and then pack the medium around them. You cannot start the seeds right in the system without them growing a little bit first. They need roots. You will need to start them in cubes or even pellets first.
- Step 14: Top it with water for the first few days to make sure that it does not dry out.
- Step 15: If you find that the amount of water

remains in the bottom of your tray after the draining cycle has ended, you will need to raise your pots up from the bottom so that they will not sit in the water that is standing. Put something below them. Do not use any bricks.

- Step 16: Plug the pump into the timer and then set it to fill three times a day for only 15 minutes on the cycle. Good times are six in the morning, noon, and six in the evening. Let your plants rest through the night.

- Step 17: The pump with air stone will stay on consistently. This oxygenates the solution and will keep it from being stagnant.

Chapter 6. Different Types of Hydroponics Garden

Now that you know a little bit about what hydroponics is it is time to learn about the different types of systems. These systems come in many different structures; some may be in large tubs, trays or towers depending on the type you want to use.

There are two basic types of systems; one is a solution system that uses water and a nutrient solution. There is no other medium used, this system is just like when you grow a potato in a cup. The plant roots will grow directly into a nutrient rich solution. The second type of system is known as the aggregate system.

In an aggregate system a medium such as sand, gravel or perlite is used and the plants roots grow into it. Both systems have to have a large amount of water and they both have to have a nutrient rich solution and they have to have oxygen. Different types of plants will do better in different systems and we will learn which ones should be grown in each system as we go through them.

There are several different hydroponic systems that you can use, they are called ebb and flow, static solution, continuous flow, aeroponics, passive sub-irrigation, run to waste, deep water, fogponics, and rotary.

The ebb and flow system is the simplest form of hydroponics and it is recommended that if you have never used hydroponics system before that you start out with this one. This one works with 2 trays or tubs. One will be placed on top of the other. The top tub will contain a medium such as gravel the bottom tub will contain a nutrient rich solution mixed with water.

The plants are planted into the top tub and using a pump the nutrient solution is periodically pumped into the top tub filled with the medium. You will use a run off of some type so that if the top tub fills up too much while the pump is pumping, the nutrient rich solution will simply drain back into the bottom tub. After the top tub has been filled with the solution it will slowly drain back into the bottom tub and the process will start again.

The pros of an ebb and flow system are that it is easy to

build; most of these can be made at home using materials that you already have or can purchase for a low price. This system is also easy to maintain. It does not require a lot of technical knowledge and if you purchase the system it is basically a plant and grows system.

This type of system provides a huge amount of nutrients to the plants since it is always filling up with the nutrient rich solution and provides as much water to the plants as they need. This is especially good for growing plants such as strawberries that need a lot of water.

This system is usually the cheapest type of system to purchase and if you are building it yourself it is also extremely cheap.

The down side of using this type of system is that you have to be very careful that your pump does not go out. If a pump was to go out and the plants were to be without water and nutrients for as few as a couple of hours the plants will die. Another con of this system is that over time with the constant filling and draining of water, salt can build up on the roots of the plants causing them to not be able to absorb the nutrients they need.

You also have to monitor the PH levels very carefully when

using an ebb and flow system because since the water is constantly flowing into the top tub and draining back into the hold tank, the PH levels can change drastically. If this is not monitored it can cause your plants to not be able to absorb the nutrients they need thus killing them.

A static solution system is when plants are grown in a container of nutrient rich solution. This system is much like growing a potato in a cup but you can use any container, buckets, tubs or jars. This is usually used for indoor growing but can also be used outdoors. If you are using a container that is clear you will need to cover it to reduce the chances of algae growing. Many people choose to use black plastic to cover their containers. If algae grow, it will take all of the nutrients out of the solution as well as all of the oxygen therefore killing your plants.

The containers that you will use will be called your reservoirs, you can have one plant per reservoir or multiple plants but you must keep in mind that as the plants grow they will need bigger reservoirs.

It is important that your plants have enough oxygen. Since your nutrient rich solution will not be flowing you will need to add oxygen to your water. You can do this by simply using an aquarium pump. Another thing you will have to do is make sure that you are changing out the solution on a regular basis. This can be done on a schedule or when the nutrient levels fall below what is desired. You have to do this because if you allow the plant to suck up all of the nutrients in the water and never replace them than your plants will die. The water has to be changed on a regular basis because there are nutrients in the water that the plant needs. Not doing so will only cause the plant to be nutrient deficient.

A continuous flow system is the next system I want to discuss. In this system the nutrient rich solution continuously flows past the roots of the plants. This system is much easier than using the static system because you are able to check the PH levels as well as the temperature of the water in the large storage tank which the water flows out of. You also don't have to worry about changing multiple containers since there is only one tank of solution for the entire system.

Another variation of this system is to allow a small amount of nutrient rich solution to flow through a shallow area where the roots will form a thick mat. These roots will absorb all of the nutrient rich solution the plants need but the top portion of the roots will be out of the solution allowing them to absorb as much oxygen as they need.

To properly design a system like this you will have to ensure that it is set on a slope; you will have to ensure that the correct slope is being used as well as the correct flow rate. It is important to note that it has been reported that when a channel is longer than 12 meters long plants have a much slower growth rate.

This system is also very cheap to use and it like the ebb and flow system has a grow bed that is separated from the reservoir. Many people will put fish in the reservoir and this is called aquaponics. Aquaponics is much more complicated than hydroponics because you have to ensure that you have the correct amount of fish or your plants will end up over fed and unable to clean the water or they will end up underfed and die. We are not going to go into depth about aquaponics but it is an option if you use a separate tank as a reservoir for your water and one for your grow bed.

The down side of this system is that the plants roots can become water logged. Water can also become stagnant in the system because the flow will move around any blockages that are created by the roots.

Aeroponics is the next type of system I want to talk about. When you are using this system, the roots of the plant will be continually misted with a nutrient rich solution. When you use this system, the plants are suspended in a container of nothing but air, the sprayers will mist the roots providing them with enough nutrients but ensuring that they do not become water logged as well as ensuring that the plants do not drown.

One of the great benefits to this type of system is that unlike many of the other systems, any type of plant can be grown using aeroponics. Since the plants are able to receive 100 percent of the oxygen, carbon dioxide and nutrients that it needs, the rooting time is reduced which allows the plant to grow larger more quickly and produce much larger fruit.

Another great benefit to this type of system is that the plants will not suffer shock if they are transplanted into soil unlike when the other hydroponic systems are used.

Passive sub-irrigation is another system that you can use to grow your plants. This system is used when a porous material is used to transport the water and nutrients to the root of the plant by absorbing it from the reservoir.

This system is great for plants that need a lot of oxygen to their roots and it also is reduces the chances of root rot because just like if the plant were in soil the roots have to work to get the water and nutrients.

A run to waste system is much like ebb and flow system meaning that the plants are in a tub and the nutrient rich solution is pumped from the reservoir into the growing tub. The difference is that once the nutrients have been depleted from the water instead of just turning it into waste, the water is processed through a filtration system so that it can be used multiple times. This system also waters from the top unlike when you use the ebb and flow system which waters from the bottom of the system.

Perlite and sand are popular mediums that can be used in this type of system and is great to grow plants such as tomatoes, cucumbers and various peppers in.

A deep water system is when the roots of the plant are suspended in water that is nutrient rich and is oxygenated. You will need to put an air pump in the water to ensure that the plant is able to get enough oxygen and does not drown. You also have to be careful when using this type of system to ensure that the roots do not become water logged. This type of system is known for producing much larger plants because of the large amount of oxygen that the plant is able to absorb from the water.

Fogponics is when the nutrients and water are transferred to the plant in the form of vapor, thus the name "fog"ponics. You will use the concept of growing the plant in a container with nothing as a medium but air just like when you use areoponics but the plants will be misted with a vapor using a timer.

As you can see there are many different types of hydroponics systems for you to choose from and you may be wondering exactly how you will choose which system will work best for you. You will need to look at the amount of money you are willing to spend, your specific needs depending on what type of plant you are growing, for example none of the systems that use sprayers work well with organic plants because the organic plant food tends to clog up the sprayers.

You will also want to look at how much experience you have with hydroponics. If you are a beginner I suggest that you start out with simple ebb and flow system and see if that works out for you. If on the other hand you have been using hydroponics for a while you can use a more complicated system.

Finally you want to look at the amount of time that you have to spend maintaining the system as well as the plants. If you have a lot of time to focus on the system you may choose to go with a manual system where you will be manually feeding and watering the plants on a schedule, if you don't have the amount of time needed for that you will want to go with an automated system but you take the risk of it breaking and your plants dying.

No one can tell you which system you need to choose because it all depends on what you want to put in, but by using the information I have just given you, you will be able to make the right choice for you, your plants, and your lifestyle.

Chapter 7. Best Plants for Hydroponics

There was never a better time to grow your own vegetables than now. Growing them is easy and can be achieved anywhere in your yard, and it is even possible to grow herbs and smaller plants on your balcony or on an apartment window.

Modern methods of farming are rapidly growing less tasty vegetables. For other reasons than taste and nutritional content, plants are cultivated, i.e., their ability to survive intact transport and yield the highest harvest possible. From the farmer's point of view, this has a negative effect on your cooking. Of course, you can choose to buy organic vegetables in the grocery store instead of everyday items, but it's difficult to find, and typically much more expensive.

You have complete control of what appears on the dinner table by increasing your own. You know exactly how new they are, what pesticides have been used to cultivate them, and how exactly they are–if a vegetable has no appeal to the broad market today, the chances to find it in a supermarket are small.

Don't worry; if you don't have sizeable garden-vegetable gardening is as effective in containers and pots as in gardens. Planting in containers in many respects is safer if you expand to a small extent, because the cups can be moved around the garden or the courtyard according to the environment, and if you encounter an unseasonable freeze, you can cover the crops before the damage occurs. Some vegetables can be grown in a tub, also more massive such as pumpkins and squash.

Another way to grow vegetables on an allowance or in a community garden if you have limited space. Allotments are small parcels of land that you rent to grow vegetables or plants. They are very common in the UK and Europe, but they can also be found all over the west, mostly funded by municipalities.

You might well think you don't know how to grow vegetables at home-at this point, this can be accurate, but you can learn. You will soon reap the rewards of your own plot of plants.

It won't take much time to gather a lot of useful information about growing vegetables, and there's nothing better than experience to support you on the path to a perfect garden.

You will need to learn other things related to your situation in order to grow vegetables at home. For example, how much sun does your selected area get every day? What are the conditions of your soil? By purchasing a simple kit from your local garden center or nursery, you can quickly determine the terms of your property. You can choose the right fertilizer for your specific soil conditions once you learn this.

Everything tastes as good as the vegetables you grew at home! If you buy it from the local store, it won't be new, and it won't take long before it begins to lose its flavor. Compare this to the vegetable garden before you cook your dinner, pick your desired food, harvest, wash and prepare it, and serve it with your meal what's fresher than that.

You should be able to enjoy healthy vegetable crops from your home vegetable garden, and you could quickly stop buying veg throughout the year. With today's economic climate this is an excellent bonus-so you won't just eat healthier food, have better tastes of vegetables, but you can save money!

It is a comfortable yet insightful introduction to people who are entirely new to gardening and want to grow vegetables. It offers step-by-step guidance for beginners who direct the reader through the selection of an appropriate plant selection area. This also presents several practical and theoretical vegetable tips growth and highlights some of its advantages in terms of money-saving and enhanced relaxation.

Now you understand which plants you would like to grow. Have seeds to buy. There are many sites on the topic, from garden centers to news agencies. Typical vegetable seeds are pretty cheap, usually under two or three pounds. Nevertheless, the number of seeds in a packet varies considerably depending on the type of plant. One packet of carrot seeds, for example, can contain about 100 grains, while a pack of boot seeds can contain only about 20. Such difference is generally proportional to the germination rate, with significantly fewer carrot seeds germinating than bean seeds.

Once you have the seeds, the next step is to plant them. This is usually the working part of the process. Many seed packs will have simple seeding, maintenance, and harvesting instructions for the crop that you plan to produce. If you have no guidance, there is plenty of valuable information on the Internet, and your nearest bibliothèque is also an excellent resource. There are numerous types of vegetables, and the demands and difficulties associated with each of them could fill up many books, so the rest will concentrate on general growth tips, rather than discussing all of these.

The soil it cultivates is one of the most elements of a plant's performance in its fundamental climate. The

identification of your soil type and the compatibility with your plants can make a real difference in its growth. Nevertheless, the introduction of some fertilizer from a garden center will alter its characteristics and make a significant difference in plants ' health. This issue coincides with feeding plants as they grow. It is important to focus on the feed given to the plants you plan to eat, so what you put on the roses may not be so good if you eat! There are several different organic feeds for very healthy vegetable plants. An interesting experiment is to purchase some and test them on a few of the same plants to see the output differences.

Another animal is eating it before you are one of the biggest problems with growing vegetables. There are main ways of avoiding this: planting greenhouse. You can or growing the vegetables in a

grow vegetables in your house, particularly if you have a conservatory, and it can be a great project for young children. The dirt and dead leaves that inevitably lead to the carpet and prevent most people from doing so at any point throughout the house. Greenhouses are an excellent alternative as they allow you to protect your plants from virtually any insect, but are costly and not always viable.

WHY GROW VEGETABLES AT HOME?

Take good care of your soil when planting vegetables to boost growth.

You're going to have to get rid of weeds. You will also want to break up the soil in order to allow air to reach and conserve humidity. It is challenging to keep up with plants if you let them get out of control. Weed every day to save extra work for yourself. Weeds steal food from your plants just another excuse to take it away from your yard!

Moisture and heat are allowed to break up the soil with a hoe. Both enable the plants to grow nutrients. Loose soil helps to breathe the plants. Plants require water. Plants need water.

The water that reaches the ground starts to evaporate as soon as it rains. When you continuously loosen the top inch of the soil, a dusty protective layer will be formed on the top, which helps to trap moisture below.

It takes some work to weed the lawn. When you keep up with the weeds, you're much better off. The best weed time is when the field is soft (as when it rains). For soft soil, you can extract the weeds from the roots.

By working between rows with a hoe, you can speed up the weeding cycle. Close the plants and keep a small quantity by hand so that you don't harm plants. It will also help if you split the soil and just start to spring out any new weeds. You save a lot of extra time in the garden with a wheel hoe. Use the wheels as your guide if you use them, and the blades will follow the same path.

Rotate your crops season after season will help you make the most of your soil. Do not plant vegetables from the same family straight after each other for the best results. Vegetables such as maize should be planted after deep rooting plants. After the root crops, vines or leaf crops will arrive. The fast-growing crops are better cultivated after those that take the garden every year.

SEED GROWING VEGETABLES

Most household gardeners prefer seed vegetables. It is much cheaper than buying seedlings because a seed kit costs just a few bucks, and you get tons of seeds. This means that every plant would cost only a few cents and, in most cases, less than one cent.

There are two ways to grow seed vegetables. You can either sew them straight into your vegetable patch or begin them in small containers and transplant them into the vegetable garden patch once they are a few centimeters high.

The first way to plant seed vegetables is called direct seeding. For succeed in this process, you must first prepare the soil. Dig up and churn the ground until it is dry, crumbled. You can also apply lime, slow-release fertilizer, and some compost and thoroughly stir in the soil.

The next move is to use your hand or stick to make a shallow trench in the soil. Most seeds do need their own soil thickness when covered in, so do not dig the trench too profoundly. Place the seeds in a shallow trench at a distance given for the plant that is shown on the back of the seed packet. After the seeds are put at the prescribed intervals, cover the seeds, and soften the soil. Once your seeds are seeded, water them gently, but make sure that you don't dislodge the seeds.

The second alternative you have for seed crops is to seed it in containers and surgery to remove into a vegetable garden. There are many containers that can be used out there, and most are just perfect. One great idea is to use old cartons to grow seed vegetables, only put one or two holes in each of the twelve spaces. Old egg cartons are perfect too, as you can just take each punnet apart and plant them into the veggie patch, and the cup breaks down when the plant grows out.

 As mentioned, any form of the container will do the job, but make sure you put a few holes in the ground.

Another perfect way to grow seeds is to buy a seed starter kit. This will send you all you need to do quickly. This is an excellent investment because it provides a perfect germination environment. There is usually a plate, pans, labels, and a transparent cover. The transparent cover retains moisture levels within the starter kit, which is what your seeds are going to like. Use a seed starter kit myself, and that has given me much better outcomes, and a higher germination rate, Seed crops must not be difficult at all, and you will have vegetables on your dinner table in no time if you use those simple techniques.

YOUR OWN VEGETABLES GROWING IN YOUR HOME

Would you like to grow one own vegetables mini without a garden? You can grow nutritious, intensely flavored mini salads, bean, and micro-greens sprouts at home year-round with an indoor micro-farm. Once plants are small, there is a much higher nutritional value. In many instances, baby vegetables provide much more nutrients than those far more mature.

You have, like many others, heard of small stacking bean sprouts that you can place in your kitchen on the window. They allow you to benefit from the health benefits of eating seeds and bean sprouts that grow with them, but they do so irregularly unless you decide to set up several at a time. More often, they only deliver interesting parts to enjoy. However, these systems don't have the properties to use soil so you won't be able to grow poultry shoots, sunflower greens, or the increasingly popular wheatgrass you then can juice.

You will also find with these systems that taking care of the mini plantlets can be a challenge to provide the nutrients you need to improve your health. When you want to use daily bubble jars or sprouts, you will spend time rinsing and watering them periodically. And if you are someone who is away from home all day because of work, it will be even more challenging to grow these kinds of crops successfully.

So, what should you do if you have little room and want to be able to grow healthy sprouts and microgreen plants to save you money in a store?

There is one way that you can grow many organic beans, sprouts, pea shoots, micro salads, and sunflower greens successfully throughout the year with little or no effort on your part. You don't even have to use artificial lighting or advanced, temperature-controlled indoor spaces, which rely on hydroponics and artificial lights. The solution we address below is one that needs very little space, no electricity, or an abundant water supply or environmental lighting.

The Easy Green Makes It Easy Grown is a fully automated self-contained hydroponic system that allows you to develop your favorite sprouts efficiently so that the health benefits of these plants are harvested and modified. The machine is one box and gives you the opportunity to grow daily amounts not only of mini vegetables but also other crops. If you are a chef, this system will allow you to make edible quality garnishes, baby salads, and microgreens in your restaurant. And because the Easy Green is a modular device, it gives you the opportunity to place one tray on top of another so that you can quickly grow your favorite crops. It also helps you to grow wheatgrass to juicing, and pea shoots to garnish food and even in salads, and seed and bean sprouts, of course. In addition, the design allows you to use the soil for sunflower seeds, small salad leaves, and micro-herbs to add flavor to your foods. Yes, the foods that can be produced using this method are almost infinite.

How does it work?

The Easy Green uses some of the most advanced hydroponic techniques. Each device is straightforward. -the box is divided into two parts (rectangular in shape). The more significant part in the production of crops, while the smaller component is the water source. Every device also has a transparent polycarbonate cover, which ensures that enough light is able to reach plants as they grow. It comes with a timer system that allows you to determine when crops are to be watered, and so you decide precisely how much water and when the plants are to grow.

Since each Easy Green Farm is fitted with different growing trays, you can customize the living rooms to suit your particular needs and mix and match the crops you develop. Baby salad vegetables or wheatgrass should be used in large trays for people who wish to grow sunflower sprouts. Nonetheless, if you want to build a large variety of crops at any given time, the smaller plates are perfect and can grow up to 10 of them.

 Simplicity means success. Another specialist pump that produces a highly oxygenated ultrasound mist of water in each Easy Green growing system creates the perfect atmosphere in which your crops can grow. Furthermore, since this system makes sure that all seeds are appropriately watered, there is no requirement that you pre-soak the seeds before putting them in the tray and yet they grow much faster than if you were planting them conventionally. The oxygen levels in the nebula are so high that it is beneficial to the young plant roots as they grow. You are also in charge of the pump in the growing chamber so that the tray is adequately ventilated, so new clean filtered air is capable of entering it each time. The other thing to consider is that unlike other hydroponics for cultivation in this one, there is no water jets or dripper nozzles that can be blocked over time.

When it comes to where your decision comes from and how you add nutrients like kelp to the reservoir to boost crop fertility when you are ready for harvest. You can determine when the watering takes place during the day and night and can break in 16-minute intervals. Once the seed has grown, the Easy Green Farm System is mounted in the tanks, and the reservoir is filled with water and left to its best effect. It is perfect for those who lead safe but very hectic lives because it can do it. To order to ensure that it works effectively, however, one must keep in mind that water in the reservoir is continuously supplied, and crops are harvested on a regular basis at their most delicious and nutritious stage of growth.

Another feature you will find with this kind of system, unlike the many other hydroponic systems available, is that soil or compost can be used there. It enables you to create the perfect atmosphere for growing crops that need to be grown longer, including sunflower greens, wheatgrass, and baby salads. This is, of course, one of several greatest of all hydroponic systems available now, allowing you to grow all sorts of germs and mini-plants in it. And make sure you get regular food supplies to improve your health conveniently

Chapter 8. Nutrient Solutions

Hydroponic nutrients could be a complex issue or as simple as pouring and mixing. The people who are new to hydroponics and are not familiar with the fertigation techniques, follow the template on the medicine. It will make you learn how to use the nutrients to provide it to the plants.

So the main questions about hydroponic nutrients when you are a beginner could be choosing your fertilizer? What nutrients should you add? How often and how much you have provided nutrients to your plants?

Let us first find out how to choose your fertilizer. Mixing hydroponic nutrients can surely be a breeze. When you are about to select your fertilizer, there are two deciding factors, i.e., wet vs. dry. Also, what plants are you growing inside that set up is essential, based on which you need to disperse the nutrients to all plants. Different nutrients are required for different plants. If you are growing commercially, dry fertilizers will be appropriate for you.

The nutrients like NPK (Nitrogen, Phosphorous, and

Potassium) which are known to be macronutrients are required by almost every type of plant. NPK comes in dozens of different ratios as plants with distinctive properties, and variety requires different proportions of NPK and other micronutrients. For example- Capsicum requires more calcium, while Cucumber requires magnesium in larger quantity.

Different mixes will give you a different product altogether. For example 13 0 45 (NPK) has 13% of nitrogen, no phosphorus, and 45% of potassium, which makes this product called potassium nitrate. Whereas, 0 0 50 (NPK) has no nitrogen, no phosphorus, 50% of potassium, and this product is called as Potassium sulfate.

Usually, for hydroponic use, you need four nutrients mixed regularly to fertilize your plants. These are-

1) NPK mix (Of different types depending upon the plant)

2) Magnesium sulfate

3) Calcium Nitrate

4) Sulfur

5) Other micronutrients solution (If needed such as iron,

zinc, copper, manganese, etc.)

Your plants will claim Oxygen, Carbon, and hydrogen from the air and water around them. The rest, you will be using in your nutrient mix, including NPK, calcium, magnesium, sulfur, and other micronutrients fertilizer which is readily available in the market.

How much and how often you should provide nutrients to the plants?

You need to check the label on the nutrient mix and follow that instruction to check how much you ought to provide that specific nutrient to the plants. For example- while you are giving magnesium sulfate, you need to check the label for ensuring the appropriate dosage required per plant.

You need to make sure what is your nutrient level of the plant before giving any nutrient mix. Top off your systems after a few days at a fixed interval and then disperse nutrients to compensate for both the dilution of the top off and the plant use.

Like any other system, hydroponics system is also a great combination of various equipment and elements. The process of hydroponic involves the soilless growing of plants with the help of water, nutrient solutions, light and many other things like water pump which generate the oxygen and tubes which is very useful for dripping water and nutrients in the roots of plants.

The growing mediums are those which things which provide external support to the plant's roots like sand or clay. And nutrient solutions are immensely responsible for the healthy and rapid growth of the plant. And in terms of lighting, these are artificial lights which work as the permanent back up of natural sunlight for the plant.

Nutrient solutions are one of the most significant parts of the hydroponic system or soilless growing process. These nutrient solutions are readily available in gardening centers, nurseries, and any farming shops. Nutrient solutions are a mixture of many nutrients like potassium, magnesium, calcium, nitrogen, and many other minerals.

However, the use of the nutrients solution solely depends on the types of plants we are growing and what sort of medium and hydroponic system we are using. Though, the nutrients must be mixed or soluble in water only then they will work or produce results. On the other hand, the composition of nutrient solution is essential, and 20 above elements will be needed to grow a plant healthy. Though, oxygen, carbon, and hydrogen are consumed from the air and water.

And rest of the nutrients elements are known as a mineral nutrient that will be dissolved by the grower, and they needed to be in an appropriate ratio. An excellent hydroponic nutrient consists of nutrients like nitrogen, copper, zinc, iron, Sulphur, Molybdenum, magnesium, potassium, chlorine, and boron.

In every greenhouse Hydroponic system, dozens of insect pests or you can say crop diseases affect it. No garden lover enjoys to use agrichemical, but, it becomes necessary to control that pest; otherwise, there is a risk of losing a crop.

In reality, the main reason why Hydroponic garden has access to a large number of insects or pest is an isolated area by which various types of insects spread quickly, and sometimes it is overwhelming.

But, this prevention is the answer. Nowadays, it has become very easier to prevent insect and control them from your Hydroponic garden.

Before knowing how to prevent and control the pest, you have to know about what are the common insect problems in Hydroponic?

1. Aphids

They usually find food around the stem and can be black, green, or greyish color. Aphids easily attract the plants which are a week or stressed. However, they are soft, pear-shaped insects with wings sap from all parts of the plant.

The worst thing is it spread the virus from one plant to another.

Prevention

The overfed plants are easily attracted to aphids. Always offer organic plant food to plants.

Solution

Use insecticidal soap to control aphids from becoming extra vulnerable.

Ensure that you will not bring anything from outside near to hydroponic plants as aphids are found in the outdoor environment.

2. Whiteflies

They look tiny moths and quickly fly away when you try to catch them. They suck the juices of the plant in every stage so that it will not grow.

Before they started feeding, they exude a sweet fluid which is also called honeydew. The sign of the whiteflies can be seen when you see the mold on the leaves of the plants.

How to prevent it?

In your hydroponic grow room, you can release parasitic wasps which mainly prey on whitefly nymphs. Time to time, you have to scrape the tiny eggs from below the leaves.

Resolutions

The solution for this is placing a few sticky traps which have the capability

3. Spider mites

They are very, very small in size even more modest than whiteflies and are the most dangerous infestation for your Hydroponic system. They are of various colors like pale green, yellow, reddish and they suck the juices of the plants from the stem.

If on the leaf top you can see the yellow speckles then it is a sign of spider mites.

Prevention

They usually occur in dry conditions, so keep the humidity level up to 50% which best suits for every plant.

Solution

Pyrethrum is a naturally occurring substance in chrysanthemums is recommended for organic farming. Its main work is to paralyze the bugs and stop spider mites feeding. Keep in mind that spider mites quickly go from one plant to another, so isolate infested plants as soon as possible.

4. Fungus gnats

Fungus Gnats is not harmful, but its larvae can damage the plants. It can be found in the roots of the plants. It looks similar to whiteflies, but their color is dingy gray.

Prevention

You can use moss or algae killing treatment to clear the algae system in which larvae can feed on them.

Solution

Try to capture the flying adults with the help of a sticky trap.

Spray with a mixture of neem oil, pyrethrum, and insecticidal soaps.

Keep in mind that this insect can lay an egg on hundreds so never ever ignore this issue of pest.

5. Thrips

Thrips look like aphids which turn the leaves into yellow or brown color. It is another juice sucker pest which mainly targets flowers, and if they feed on petals or leaves, they become dark and brittle.

They bore holes and usually insert their eggs in leaves and stems.

Prevention

Just shake the plant gently, which stirs up Thrips. It's egg look like a minor pimple on the leaves so crush them with a finger.

Solution

It gets easily trapped in the sticky trap so you can dispose of them by this method. On the other hand, you can use potassium salts acids which easily wash them off from the leaves. Moreover, the life cycle of thrips is concise, so you have to repeat the application of salt 3-4 times within a span of 10 days.

Now you will come to know various preventive measures by which you can control these pests. They are: -

1. First and foremost, the thing you can do and which is also the best means to maintain a healthy garden is cleanliness.
2. Before entering into the garden, wash your hands and even coming between the crops.
3. In your Hydroponic grow area to remove all the dead leaves and debris which are scattered as most of the insects and pests come on dead and decayed matter.
4. If there is any dead plant or it is decaying with time, dispose them off.
5. For your Hydroponic grow area keep a separate set of tools like trowel or pruners. Most fundamentally, don't use these tools on your houseplants or plants which are outside as insects ride from plant to plant.
6. Clean the tools while dipping into the isopropyl alcohol.

Various other preventive measures which are very crucial: -

1. Keep the humidity of the place around 50-60% and keep the hydroponic garden cool that is 75 degrees.
2. There should be proper ventilation and regular air movement as it prevents mold and funguses.
3. Make sure you don't overwater the plants which again can create mold, mildew, and algae.
4. When you are working on outdoor crops, never come directly to indoor plants. Instead, do it reverse.
5. Don't come directly to your indoor garden after visiting the plant nursery.
6. Don't smoke inside the grow room as plants can catch a virus.
7. Always use yellow or blue sticky cards so that you come to know the number of pests around the plants.
8. Ensure that when you enter the garden, always wear sterile clothes.
9. Don't bring anything into your hydroponic area, which is not clean or contaminated.

10. Whenever you are trying a new plant in the growing area, to be careful as it can bring various pests and insects with them as it is coming from outside.

What are the measures you can take if there is a pest or insects in your hydroponic growing area which can damage the plants?

If you have noticed that pests or insects are there on the plants you need to fix it quickly; otherwise, it will harm the plants abruptly. However, once pest had made its way to the plants, it becomes challenging to mitigate the issue. The speed of pests or insects is so fast that if one plant is affected other will for sure get affected.

1. Don't take care of the pest

Acting immediately will save your plants before it gets damaged.

2. Determine what type of intervention is needed

Some of the pests or insects can be taken care of as the environment changes, manly removal, various other methods, but some can only be banished only with chemicals. But make sure that you don't use chemicals into your hydroponic system.

3. Handpick them

Some of the pests or insects are very big as you can pick them with your hands like caterpillars, beetles, slugs. Try to squash them or drop them in soapy water.

4. Spray them with water

Few of the pests can easily be knocked with the help of water but make sure you spray the water underside the leaves.

5. Try a pheromone trap

This trap is commercially produced by the people which is coated with sex hormones and few fragrances by which small insects get attracted towards it. This trap can only work in an indoor area, not in the outdoor garden.

6. Use insecticides or fungal spray

Make sure that you use the least toxic spray, which does less harm to the pests or insects as saving the environment is our priority.

7. Spider mulch

Another way to save your plants from pests or insects is offering spider mulch to them to hide which is made up of straw or dried grass. With this, every type of pests will be under control.

One crucial thing to be noted that while setting up, spider mulch is set around the plants but doesn't allow debris to accumulate.

Well, all the above prevention and control measures need to be implemented strictly if you want that your hydroponic garden will not get any pests or insects. Moreover, any of the products which you are using on your organic plants should be branded in order to make them safe and healthy.

Chapter 9.   Nutrient

Water is the essential ingredient of all life, and it has an especially vital role in the life of plants. Water is a reliable vehicle that provides the transport of nutrients and energy (salts and sugars) to the cells within a plant. Unfortunately, the soil and environment that plants generally grow in are far from perfect. Therefore, the goal with hydroponics is to try to replicate what occurs in a perfectly natural and optimal growing setting. This is achieved by consistently enriching the water with nutrients, and then making these available for absorption by our plants. We refer to this water as a balanced 'nutrient solution.'

The nutrient solution that you will supply is generally provided through a human-made embedded system. This gives rise to the benefit of avoiding the evaporation that occurs in soil. In other words, we're ensuring that this nutrient-rich water is always available to our plants when they require it. Whether you know it or not, you've likely already practiced simple hydroponics by putting flowers in a vase and adding a ready-made nutrient solution.

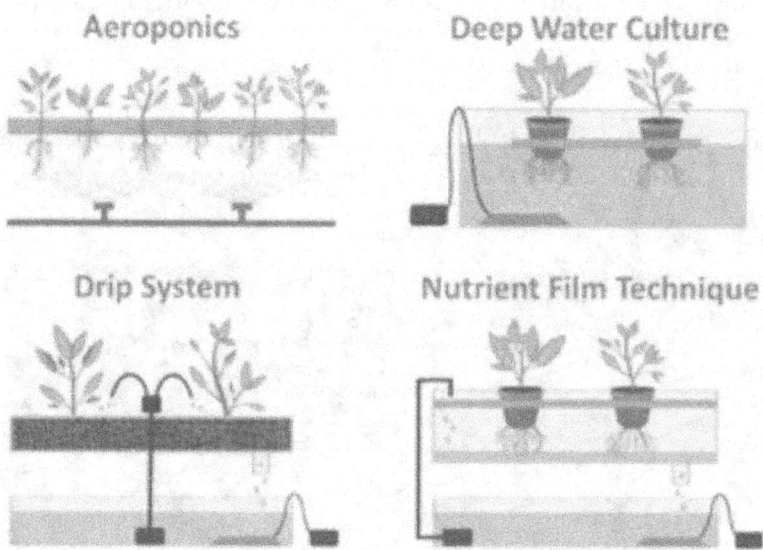

Hydroponics is consistently growing in popularity in the modern world, from backyard ventures to hydroponic applications on space stations! Hydroponics will play a key role in being able to provide nutrition as humans continue to explore the possibility of living on other planets. On a more fundamental level, hydroponics offers an affordable means of producing food for low-income areas of the world and the popularity of growing hydroponically as a hobby has gained a fair deal of popularity over recent decades.

A great way to describe hydroponic gardening is to say that it is a soil-free type of gardening. Great leaps in technology have allowed plants to grow without soil. However, this unique way of planting that is rapidly becoming popular has been around for decades.

This is the Hanging Gardens of Babylon. These early forms of hydroponic gardening were placed on top of ziggurats, which were watered through dividing channels, and supplied with water from the Euphrates River.

Ancient Mexico also had its version of hydroponic gardening. Floating gardens, or chinampas, are gardens with plants grown in a lake in ancient Mexico.

However, the ultimate origin of hydroponic gardening occurs in nature itself. No human interference or structures took place in this naturally produced hydroponic garden.

For example, orchids are the most significant examples of hydroponic gardening. They have aerial roots that innately do not need soil to thrive.

Hydroponics is seen as the next step in the evolution of agriculture by many experts as it has revolutionized the ability to grow plants and crops. It is most often used in greenhouses to experiment with and grow different varieties of plants. Hydroponics is revolutionary because it eliminates the need for what was considered a major element for growing plants and crops, namely soil.

There are three components that plants require to grow correctly i.e., water, air (oxygen and carbon dioxide), and soil.

The principle behind hydroponics is that soil provides the mineral nutrients required by plants as well as the solid medium in which they "anchor" their roots. However, it has been discovered that plants can absorb the minerals and nutrients required for proper growth from liquid medium and solutions.

Hydroponics is becoming a widely accepted technique for growing healthy and nutritious vegetables, fruits, and flowers both indoor and outdoor. It also provides us the most robust crops containing the highest number of vitamins, minerals, and nutrients and that too in a minimum space. Today, many farmers worldwide are using hydroponics for producing fruits, vegetables, and flowers because of the technique's ability to produce rich nutrients and minerals and high yields. Many farmers are claiming that their production capacity has increased many-fold after using hydroponics.

Today, we are becoming more prone to diseases, and we are putting a substantial amount of chemicals and pesticides inside our body using traditional farming products. These agricultural products have such a large amount of chemicals that some physicians have proscribed their use in some patients suffering from diabetes, high blood pressure, and allergies. Now, many people are diverting to natural forms of cultivation such as organic farming and hydroponics. If you have a small family and you think that traditional food products are harming your health, then hydroponics is the best way to provide a regular source of fruits and vegetables rich in nutrients, vitamins, and minerals. You can quickly grow them on your property with very little space and minimum investment. Hydroponics is also a great way for some commercial farmers and nursery owners to increase their profit and sales.

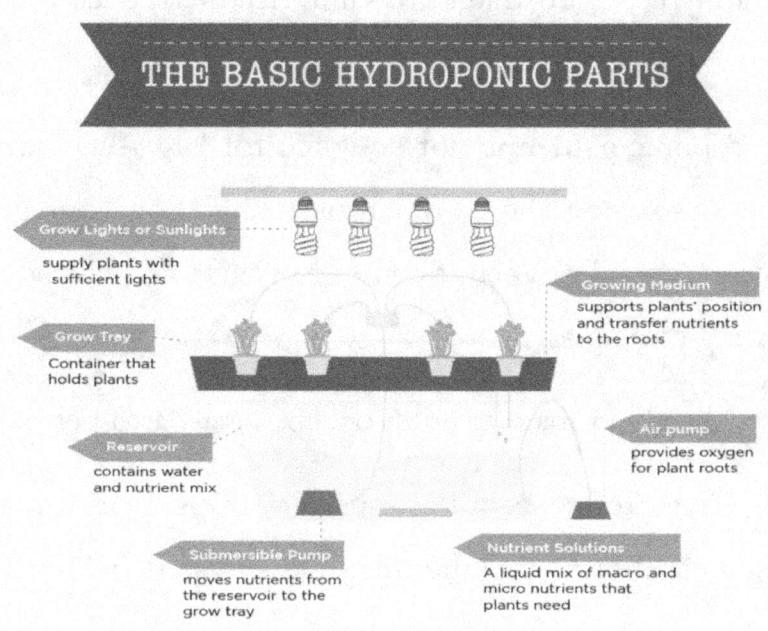

A simple hydroponic system typically contains the following essential elements:

Nutrient solution: A solution of water, essential nutrients, and oxygen supply that directly comes in contact with the roots of your hydroponic plants.

Plant holding material: This comprises a holding cup; containing holes to supply essential nutrients, and a base in which these cups should be placed.

Substrates: In hydroponics, soil is not used; therefore there must be a substrate to hold the plant firmly for growth. Some commonly used substrates are sand, rice husk, coconut fiber, and volcanic stones.

A hydroponic garden is not designed for large-scale farming activities, so your choice of crops to have on your garden matters. Generally, when it comes to vegetables, consider the following principles:

- Choose crops that don't occupy a vast area per plant.

- Give preference to fast-growing crops, especially those that take about 3 to 4 months or less to start yielding.

- If you are planting crops that take longer to mature, they should be those that continue to give yields over a long period of time.

- Consider crops that do not have a wide canopy so that you can have variety in your garden. A canopy will deny other plants much-needed sunlight to grow well.

Chapter 10.   Most common Problems

Our time together has almost come to a close. Before you go out and get going on your own garden, let us take the time to look at some of the mistakes and myths that pop up frequently in discussions on hydroponic gardening. By digging through the myths to find the truth and learning from the mistakes of those that came before us, we are able to benefit from the knowledge and avoid making the same mistakes ourselves.

Mistake: Hard-to-Use Setups

When you are setting up your hydroponic garden, it is important that you consider how hard it will be to use. Are you going to have a difficult time reaching the plants in the back because you put the garden up against a wall? Are you going to bump into the lights every time you try to tend the bed because the space is too small and cramped?

When you are setting up your garden it is important that you consider issues such as the physical space in which it will sit. You want to make sure that you can get to all your plants without a struggle. If you're knocking over lights or throwing your back out to reach plants, then the setup isn't going to be a very good one. Chances are you are going to end up breaking something or neglecting it. Consider the ways in which you move through the garden space; make sure that you are able to reach everything.

You also want to make sure that you are able to get to your reservoir easily. While it may be tempting just to rest the grow tray on top of the reservoir, consider how this might cause issues when it comes time to switch the nutrient solution. Will you have somewhere to place the grow tray while you have to mess around with the reservoir? If not, then how did you plan to do it?

Myth: Hydroponic Gardens Are Only for Illegal Substances

It seems that any time hydroponics pop up in the news it is in relation to some illegal grow operation that has been busted by the police. This has led to a stigma around hydroponics, one which it really doesn't deserve. Just because it happens that a lot of illegal growers use hydroponic setups, it doesn't mean that hydroponics is used just for illegal purposes.

As we saw above, we went an entire book looking at

hydroponics and never once did we mention any drugs. We looked at how hydroponics will help our herb gardens to produce 30% more aromatic oils. We talked about vegetables and fruits. Never once did we speak about illegal substances.

This is because hydroponics is a system for growing plants. Those plants don't need to be illegal. They can be, yes. But they can also be the garden veggies you serve in a salad. Hydroponics is just a great system for growing plants and it is a system that you can run from inside your house, which means that you can hide your garden easily. But hydroponics itself is not illegal, it does not mean that you are taking part in illegal activities and this particular myth should be put to rest already.

Mistake: Choosing the Wrong Crops for Your Climate

You hear about a new crop on one of the gardening sites you check online. It sounds like it could be a lot of fun to grow, some kind of berry you never heard of before and people say it does great in a hydroponic setup. You order some seeds, plant it and it grows but it just doesn't give the results you wanted. Looking to see what goes wrong, you do some more Googling on the plant and you realize it needs to be in a super-hot, arid environment. And you're living through the coldest winter of your life.

Different plants want different climates and nothing will be more disappointing than trying to grow a plant that just doesn't like the climate you can offer. We should always do our research on the plants that we want to grow. We can do this easily with Google or by going into our local hydroponic store to speak to the staff.

Myth: Hydroponics Have to be Done Indoors

We've spoken a lot about indoor hydroponics in this book. This was a choice to highlight the fact that we can raise hydroponics indoors. There any many people out there who don't have access to an outside plot in which to start a garden. Most people that live in an apartment building have at best a balcony and many don't even have that much. Being that you can have an indoor garden, hydroponics offers a way for more people to get into gardening.

But this doesn't mean that you can't have an outdoor hydroponic garden. When we raise our gardens indoors, we are able to control the seasons and really take an active role in maintaining the humidity and temperature, how long the grow lights are on and much more. If we grow outdoors, then we can save money on grow lights by using the sun but we also open our garden up to more risk from pests and disease. However, hydroponics can be done anywhere that you want.

Mistake: Picking the Wrong Plants for Your Setup

This could also be called "Not Doing Your Research." Like picking plants that match your climate, you are also going to want to make sure you pick plants that will work well in your setup. Some plants work better in different systems. Some want less water; some want slower draining and others want more water and others yet want faster draining.

It is important that you research the plants that you want to put in your garden. There are hundreds upon hundreds of websites jam-packed with information about every plant you could consider growing. They will tell you the pH and EC levels for the plant, how hot they like their environment, how much water they want and what type of hydroponic setup is best for them. We looked at a handful throughout this book but there is no way we could have covered all of them. But Google is your friend.

So make sure you do your research and plan out your garden.

Preparing yourself with information will avoid costly mistakes. Not only does it cost to grow but there is also a time cost and you will lose weeks before you realize that growing that one plant is a losing battle.

Myth: Hydroponics is Super Expensive

This myth has good reason to be around. The truth is that hydroponics can be expensive. Can be. But just because it can be doesn't mean that it always is. When you head to the hydroponic store and look at all the prices and get talked into buying more than you really needed, then it is going to be expensive. But like many hobbies, it depends on how serious you want to take it and you can always start slow.

There are a ton of ways to cut down costs when beginning your garden. Searching online you can find hundreds of do-it-yourself guides to starting a hydroponic setup. These offer great ways to try out hydroponic gardening for the new grower. You can get your hands dirty and really see if it is something that you enjoy before you go spending a lot of money. Speaking of spending a lot of money…

Mistake: Scaling Up the Operation Too Early

Starting off too big can be a terrible mistake. For one, it

means sinking a lot of money into growing right out the gate. Before you do this you should at least have some experience with hydroponics. Another big issue is that until you have some experience you don't actually know how to best care for your garden and every step in the operation cycle is going to be a learning experience. This isn't bad when we start small but starting bigger means any mistakes we make along the way are going to cost us that much more.

You should start slow and learn the ropes. As you learn the way your plants take to the system, get a feel for how they grow in your setup, then you can begin to expand. You can start to add in another grow tray, maybe two. But add slowly, take your time and make sure you have a good grasp of how to run a small garden before you jump into a large one. You can always get there but patience will help save you from some truly devastating mistakes along the way. It's one thing to mess up one grow tray, it's another to mess up a dozen.

Myth: Hydroponics is Unnatural

What happened to just stick a plant in the ground and letting it grow? Hydroponics seems like a lot of work to do the same thing. The plants come out bigger, too. Seems like there must be something unnatural going on here. It must be all those chemicals used in the solution.

Of course, this myth is just silly. We are growing plants and using natural mix in our grow trays. We mix together a nutrient solution but all of these are natural nutrients that the plants take from the Earth anyway. Hydroponics is just a system of growing. We grow healthy plants the same as any gardener tries to. There are no gross chemicals being used to give us better growth than soil. All we are doing is using the natural desires of the plant to provide it with the most comfortable growing experience we can.

In a way, hydroponics is almost like owning a pet. There are wild dogs in the world but nobody thinks it is unhealthy to have a pet dog. We are treating our plants the same; we are providing for their needs so that they can focus on living. Just in the case of plants, living means growing into fruit or vegetables that we can enjoy afterward!

Mistake: Not Maintaining Your Garden

I know, I know. You've heard this one before. But it is the number one mistake that new growers make and so we are going to speak about it one last time. The fact is that maintaining your garden doesn't just mean changing the water. It doesn't just mean we look at the garden when the plants look ill and infected and get to work. Maintaining our gardens is a commitment that any gardener has to honor.

Something spill? Better wipe that up. There's dead plant matter in your grow tray or on the floor around your setup? Best clean that up and get rid of it. Infestations and infections love to grow in these conditions. So, check your plants, test the water, clean up the beds and show them a little love. You wouldn't let your dog sleep in its own waste, so why would you let your plants? Maintaining your garden is the most important thing you can do as a new grower.

Treat your plants right.

Mistake: Forgetting to Have Fun

If you are growing because you want to sell your crops, that's a fine reason to do it. But try to have fun. For many, this is an enjoyable hobby and brings them a lot of peace. When you start to get money involved, it can be easy to lose track of that. Don't forget to take time to smell the roses. Or the tomatoes, whatever it is you're growing.

Starting Your Garden Without Proper Knowledge

Any hobby requires knowledge. Sometimes you can learn as you enjoy your hobby, but for hydroponic gardening, you will discover more fun and enjoyment if you arm yourself with the proper education first. A lot of novice gardeners start out without gathering all the information required to start, which can lead to issues with the system or proper nutrient dispersal.

Harvesting Too Early

Each plant has its own harvesting time table. A few plants will go from seed to plant to full fruit or vegetable in as little as a month. Other plants can take 70 to 120 days from germination to harvest time. It would be nice if you can start picking fruits and vegetables off the plants as soon as they appear, but you risk an immature vegetable or fruit, which can mean a poor taste. Let the fruits and vegetables grow to full maturity before picking them.

Overwatering/Under Watering

Water is a crucial element to growing your plants; however, there is a fine line between not watering enough and watering too much. The reason hydroponic systems need to have a timer is so you can regulate the watering process with more accuracy. Continually saturating the plants with water will create drooping leaves, as well as hinder the growth of the plants. Some plants will start to rot due to too much water. You also cannot let the roots get too dry. Dry roots mean not enough nutrients, plus they will shrivel up and die. A good rule of thumb is to water your plants when you see the top layer of medium become dry. Stick your finger into the medium and test whether it is wet. If it is not, then you are not watering your plants enough. Other reasons to set up your hydroponic system with drainage is to ensure your plants are not over watered. The roots can soak up what they need and the rest of the water will go back into the reservoir.

Improper Lighting

Even the best gardeners know that sometimes daylight just is not enough because it can be infrequent. The sun might be behind a cloud or it might be raining, which takes away from the proper light required for your crops. For your crop to grow to its proper height and to keep the leaves a healthy green, you have to provide proper light. Reading lights and single bulbs are not the best lamps, which most novices tend to use. Fluorescent bulbs can be okay, but they are highly expensive to run and replace. This is why it is suggested to avoid the mistake of regular lights and fluorescent bulbs in favor of using high pressure sodium or LED lights, which are more cost effective. It does not mean plants need light 24/7, but consistent light without overheating the plant is necessary.

Chapter 11. Strategies to avoid insects

The term pest control often conjures up images of people using sprays filled with chemicals. You might think that using such methods is rather extreme. But if you spot your wonderful tomatoes surrounded by ants or your beautiful flowers suddenly attacked by flies, then you might think of drowning those creatures in pesticides.

However, what might sound like a frightening scenario can typically be solved by taking a few precautionary steps. If all else fails and you still would like to consider using sprays, then do not worry.

The thing about pesticides is that they have an instant (and noticeable) effect. You can see the number of pests on your plants reduced. Nevertheless, there are certain effects in the long term – such as depleting the health of your soil and slightly poisoning your water – that might prove disastrous for you in the future. You might have to change the soil entirely. If you are using a raised bed, then this might not be a problem. However, if you have decided to plant directly into the earth, then getting rid of that entire pesticide residue is a strenuous process.

Here is another thing that you should keep in mind; sometimes, getting rid of the pests may not be necessary. If you have aphids roaming around on your plants, then see if you have helpful insects that dine on these aphids. In fact, certain farmers are known to let the pests live. This is because they usually have some form of predator that can take care of the pest problem. This has two beneficial results:

- You do not have to spend time (and money, in some situations) on pest control activities.

- You let someone (or something) else take care of the problem for you. A friend in need is a friend indeed. Even if that friend just happens to have four legs, wings, or antennae.

Another thing to keep in mind; your problem might not be related to pests. It is easy to think that certain creatures have wreaked havoc on your lovely garden. Actually, it is certainly tempting to think that way. However, in many cases, the situation might just be because of other factors. Is there enough moisture for the plants? Are strong winds causing harm to them? Was there heavy rainfall recently? Did it hail? Even water pollution could be another factor to consider. You see, all of these factors cause unnecessary stress on the plants, which further begins to attract the pests in your area. Trying to get to the root of the problem might help you effectively remove the pests without using any pest control techniques (including pesticides).

The idea behind evaluating your garden is to know what kind of problem you are dealing with. That may help you decide if you would like to head over to the next step, which is the integrated pest management, or 'IPM' for short, process.

In IPM, farmers and gardeners take gradually stronger steps to get rid of the pests in their garden. They start by working on the conditions that help the growth of the crops. Are these conditions beneficial? Do the crops have everything they need? Once they are able to work around these conditions, they seek to establish a level of damage they can accept. Once that is done, they move on to using methods that have minimal toxicity. If that does not work, they begin using toxic or invasive methods.

Join the Resistance!

The first thing that you should do is focus on creating pest resistance plants. You see, gardeners and farmers often work with a plethora of plants species. Some of these plants have some unique traits. One of those unique traits is the ability of the plant to have disease resistance. This means that the plant suffers minimal damage from a specific disease, similar to how the human immune system builds resistances against diseases.

Many of the modern plants have built resistance to many diseases that could cause considerable damage. What's more, you can find plants that also have resistance to certain insects. For example, you can find special types of squash that can keep away certain types of beetles. This might help you effectively find a solution against these pests without having to resort to other methods of pest control.

In fact, when you are purchasing plants, you might receive information about what pests those plants resist. After knowing what pests are common in your area, you can match the plant to that particular pest.

Inviting Less Pests

While you might be confident that you have taken all the

precautionary steps to keep away pests, there might be certain reasons your garden is still attracting those nasty critters.

Mixed Plants

Most insects have receptors that allow them to target their favorite plants. It is how bees can seek out nectar so easily. If you have the plants that insects are waiting to attack and you have done nothing to protect those plants, then you might as well schedule buffet hours for the insects! What you can do to avoid this situation is to plant your crops in small batches throughout your garden. Then you can add other plants into the mix (preferably those that have resistance against the pests in your area). This confuses the insects, tricking them into believing that perhaps your garden does not have the food they are looking for. Additionally, you might be able to avoid diseases from spreading when you mix plant breeds.

Timing

Certain pests often arrive during certain climates. This fact might give you an idea of the kind of threat you are dealing with. When plants are young, they do not have the strength to ward off pests effectively, which is why you can plant your crops early so that by the time pest climate arrives, your crops have strong tissues. In some cases, insects often leave eggs behind in gardens. When the larvae hatch, they find a ready source of food in the plants around them. For this reason, you could also plant your crops a few weeks after the larvae have hatched, allowing you to starve the pests before working on your garden.

Here is a pro tip: speak to farmers in your area about the emergence of pests. They have extensive knowledge about when these pests might come out during a particular season, allowing you to know how long to wait before planting your crops.

Crop Rotation

You can move around the crops to new locations in your greenhouse each year. This does not give pests a particular spot to target. Shifting locations confuses the pests, who might be used to finding plants in a specific spot of the garden. Certain insects often lay their eggs in one location when they realize that they know where they can find a ready supply of food. However, by moving your crops around, larvae that hatch might not find their food source. Before they can discover food, they might starve and you might be able to get rid of them without much effort. Do note that crop rotation is most commonly possible with annual plants, when they can be cycled year after year.

Go Easy on the Fertilizer

This might be a common mistake committed by beginners. Gardeners who are starting out might worry about the amount of fertilizer that they use. Many use too much to avoid using too little. Unfortunately, too much fertilizer can cause harm to plants, just the way too little can. In fact, you could say that increasing the amount of fertilizer to a plant is like giving steroids to them! For example, soil nutrients provide nitrogen to the plant. This is good in moderate quantities. By adding more fertilizer, you increase the supply of nitrogen. Providing excess amounts of nitrogen might cause rapid growth in plants. This causes them to end up being juicy. This might not sound all that bad. Who doesn't love juicy food? You and every other multi-legged creature will be waiting to get a bite out of those plants. Pests might become attracted to the unnatural growth, finding a rich source of food for them and their offspring.

Clean Up Other Materials

If you notice fallen leaves, fruits, or other objects in your garden that should not typically be there, then make sure you clear them out. These objects and debris might carry organisms and pests on them that could be transferred to your plants. This increases the chances of infecting your plants with diseases or sending pests into their midst. Once you have cleaned up, see if you can also cultivate the soil when you get the opportunity. This reveals any hidden pest eggs. Additionally, if there are any larvae, you might just let predators (or even the weather) get rid of them.

Make Friends with Creatures

I am not asking you to invite creatures into your house for tea and supper. What I mean is to allow the growth of certain organisms that could help you get rid of pests. For example, certain types of spiders leave your plants alone, but find abundant food in the pests that might live there. You can always encourage the growth of these pest-hunters, as you can call them.

Insecticides

These are a form of pesticide that are specifically made to harm, eliminate, or repel one or more species of insect. You can discover insecticides in various forms such as sprays, gels, and even traps. Pick one based on the pest that is attacking your garden.

Once you have selected your insecticide, it is better to know the below tips:

- I would recommend using just one type of insecticide in your garden. Adding two or more insecticides diminishes their effect and may inadvertently cause harm to your garden.

- Remember that not all insecticides take the same time to remove pests from your garden. You might have to wait longer for certain types.

- Try to see if you really need the spray. For example, if you want to get rid of ants, you could use a bait instead (after all, ants are attracted to nearby sources of food).

Fungicides

These are pesticides that are made to kill fungal infections on the plants and any fungi spores that might have latched onto your crops. In some cases, fungicides are used to mitigate the effects of mildew and mold. The way they function is by damaging either the fungal cell structure or stopping the energy production in cells.

When you are ready to use your fungicide, do make note of the below tips:

- In many cases, people might accidently diagnose fungal diseases for their plants when in reality, it might not be a disease at all. Make sure you use the help of local experts to give you a second opinion. They might just prevent you from buying a fungicide needlessly and might recommend another solution.

- Make sure that leaves are not kept wet for too long. Simply keeping the leaves dry after watering them helps reduce the spread of fungi.

- Keep your tools sanitized. Sometimes, the fungi could spread from one plant to another because they stuck to the tools you were using.

Herbicides

The main purpose of herbicides in a garden is to get rid of all the weeds.

When you have gotten your herbicide, do make note of the following tips:

- Always make sure that the instructions on the herbicide suit your purposes.

- Go easy on its application. Adding more herbicide might sound like a safe bet, but it might end up damaging your plants. If you feel unsure, read the instructions provided on the herbicide to understand its usage quantity.

- Certain herbicides show immediate results. Others take a while to get rid of the weeds. Always check with the seller or supplier for details before using the herbicide. This way, you are not left wondering if you had bought a defective product when you see weeds present even after the third day of using the herbicide.

- Herbicides also have an effect on the soil, so make sure you speak to experts about your garden's soil types before you make a purchase.

Chapter 12. Safeguards

While hydroponic gardens are some of the best that you can make in terms of efficiency and how easy they are to use, there are some issues that you can come across in your first few years as you learn how to get the process down.

There are several risks that you will need to watch out for because they can hinder how well your plants are growing and flourishing. Luckily, hydroponics are easy to use and they will make it simple to avoid problems as long as you are aware and looking for them. Here are some of the issues that you can look for and try to prevent for the best hydroponic garden possible.

Algae And Fungi

If you have too much humidity near your plants, you could have issues with fungi growing. This is a delicate balance that you have to deal with. While having some humidity in place is critical for helping the plants to grow, once the levels get too high, the fungi are going to keep on growing and taking over the whole place. So make sure to watch out for the humidity levels and constantly check it.

In addition, you need to take some time to take care of your plants. Take away any dead leaves or stems from your garden so that the fungi don't have anything to feed around. You shouldn't overwater the plants or this could change the humidity levels as well.

Sometimes even your best efforts aren't going to work. Perhaps the heat and humidity outside are too high and the fungi are going to grow without you having any way to stop it. If the fungi come out during the growing system, be sure to use a high-quality fungicide that can kill it off without causing any harm to the plant. The earlier on you can catch the outbreak of fungi, the better chance you have of preventing any further issues. You can even use a cloth that is dry to help remove it if it happens to get onto a particular plant.

There is another fungus that is known to grow in the medium. You will notice that there is a thin layer on top of your growing medium. The best thing to do for this is add in a little bit more of the LECA medium onto the top of what is already there.. This is going to help soak up some of the extra moisture so you won't have to do much more to get it fixed.

Algae can take another toll on your plants and this is going to thrive when the plant receives a lot of light. It can occur in both the growing medium and the nutrient solution. The algae are going to compete with the plants to get all of the nutrient solution, making it hard for the plants to get what they need.

To prevent this issue, you should take care to prevent direct light rays from entering into the reservoir and make sure that the water never sits still or you could have some issues. If you do have some algae that come into the reservoir, you will need to stop the process and wash it out with some bleach. If the algae come along in the growing medium, you will need to wipe it all away.

Water Microbes

The next obstacle you are going to need to watch out for is water microbes. These can make your nutrient solution ineffective because they are going to mess with the solution. There are many microbes that can show up in the water and will make it lose its goodness and not work as efficiently. You will be able to tell when these harmful microbes are present in the brown roots and bad smells that occur since they are going to ruin the root systems of your plants. Usually, this occurs when the water is still and warm so you need to create the right environment that will prevent this bad stuff from happening.

The best thing that you can do to prevent these bad microbes is to keep the right temperature in the water so they can't grow. 68 to 75 degrees is a great temperature and try to not let it vary very much. A pump is a good thing to use because this keeps the water from being still and moves it all around. When the water stays still, it is going to encourage the microbes, but when it is moving, the oxygen promoted should be sufficient to deter bad microbes.

Keeping your solution in order is important and ensuring that no harmful bacteria are able to grow in the water and ruin all your hard work, make sure that you are following some of the tips above.

Pests And Diseases

Plants can suffer from a variety of diseases and can suffer an attack from pests. The elements that cause diseases in human beings and animals cause diseases, albeit of different kinds, to plants as well. These diseases can wreak havoc on your plants and your produce. Because of this, many people use all sorts of pesticides, insecticides etc. to protect their plants.

Hydroponic Gardening systems, especially the indoor gardening systems, are not that susceptible to diseases and pests because they do not come in contact with harmful elements that may cause them. There is a low chance of these elements entering your system.

The soil is considered one of the main culprits for transporting the bacteria and viruses that cause disease in plants. As hydroponic gardening is done without soil, it reduces the risk of contamination. Having said this, plants are more likely to contract disease from other plants. Plant diseases are carried from a host plant in favorable conditions.

Plants that grow outdoors in soil are also more susceptible to diseases because often they become weak due to the fluctuating environmental conditions such as too much shade, too much sun, too less water etc. Even nutrient deficiency, excessive nutrients or pH imbalance can induce disease as well. As you must have noticed, many of the above circumstances simply cannot happen in the indoor hydroponic system. Yet your plants can catch diseases through incorrect care.

There are many factors such as incorrect handling etc. that may cause your plants to suffer. One of the foremost reasons why your plants contract disease is because they are handled without being aware of hygiene. If you handle your plants and equipment without cleaning your hands, there is a high risk of contamination.

Most of these diseases need harsh chemical treatments that are not good for your plant's health in the long term. These chemicals can possess your hydroponic system and can singlehandedly destroy your harvest. Therefore, what can you do when your precious system is under attack of diseases?

Common Solution:

Instead of directly using the commercially available and harsh chemical treatments, try using simple homemade solutions. More than often these solutions clear out the infection. A solution that is popular amongst gardeners is the All Purpose Cure Solution. To make this solution you need to mix baking soda, lemon or lime juice and a drop or two of dish detergent with water. Put this solution in a bottle that has a spray nozzle and spray it generously over the affected portion of your plant. Most of the time, this solution works wonder although you have to spray it frequently. Be aware that sometimes this isn't enough. In such a case, you can try using other options such as cayenne pepper, salt etc. but be careful while using them. If nothing works, you will have to use the chemicals to save your plants.

Now let us have a look at some of the most common diseases and disorders that can affect your plants.

- Root Rot

Root rot is a kind of fungus that destroys the roots of the plants by 'rotting' them. This disease thus can kill your plants since they depend on their root system.

Treatment: You can use a mild fungicide to cure this one. Gently cut away the affected parts of the root and spray the fungicide lightly over the roots.

- Black Mold

Black mold darkens or blackens the leaf. A grayish or blackish growth is often seen on the leaves of the affected plant. This mold often results in leaf drop.

Treatment: Using a soft toothbrush, scrub off the mold gently. Clean the affected leaves with a damp cloth and with the All Purpose solution mentioned above. Once again, clean the leaves with a clean damp cloth.

- Powdery Mildew

Powdery Mildew is one of the most common diseases of plants and it is found almost in every corner of the world. This is a form of fungus and it results in whitish, grayish spots that are seen on the underside of the leaves. The leaves dry up fast and then drop off. It is commonly found in areas where the humidity is generally high.

Treatment: Although this disease is very common, fortunately, it is very easy to cure as well. Just take the All Purpose solution mentioned above and spray it all over the affected leaves. With this, if you find that your leaf is being affected with the fungus, cut the leaf off as soon as possible.

- Damping Off

Damping off is a very dangerous disease that normally only attacks plants that are planted in soil. With this disease, the fungus attacks small plants around the portion of the stem that is the nearest to the soil. The affected portion becomes weak or rots and the plant falls over and dies. This can also happen in hydroponic systems except that instead of soil the plants die in the water.

Clean the container in which your affected plant was planted before planting anything new in it.

- Anthracnose

This happens in normal circumstances when the plant is overwatered. It causes dark marks on the leaves that fry them and finally these leaves drop off.

Treatment: Cut off the damaged or affected leaf and then spray the plant mildly with a fungicide.

- Rust

This highly contagious disease occurs mostly in highly humid areas. The symptoms of this disease include raised powdery pustules. These are scarlet red in color and are commonly seen on the undersides of the leaves. These can turn the leaves yellow and can make them drop off. The plant may die too.

Treatment: This cannot be treated with simple tools and you need to use harsh chemicals to treat it. Cut off the affected leaves if they are few in number and then use chemicals like maneb or zined.

- Crown and Stem Rot

This is a very common fungus that can cause the plant to get pulpy and rot away.

Treatment: Cut off the rotten and affected area as soon as possible. Spray the plant with a fungicide.

- Botrytis

This is commonly caused because of improper and inadequate ventilation. Grayish or whitish fuzz is seen on leaves. It is very uncommon in hydroponic gardens.

Treatment: Increase the ventilation and cut off the affected parts away.

- Early Blight

This is another very harmful disease that can kill a plant. Dark brownish black spots are seen on all the parts of the plant that can weaken it completely.

Treatment: This thing cannot be treated with simple tools and you need to use harsh chemicals to treat it. Cut off the affected parts if they are few in number and then use chemicals like maneb or zined.

- Club Root

This affects the growth of the plants. The roots of the affected plants turn into weirdly shaped tubers.

Treatment: Spray with a mild fungicide.

Conclusion

Thanks for reading your entire copy of the Hydroponics: The Beginner's Guide to Effective Hydroponic Gardening at Home. Let's hope it was informative and provided you with all of the tools you need to achieve your goals of gardening at home. You should have plenty of knowledge of what type of hydroponic system will best suit your space, budget, and time.

Once you have the perfect selection for your space, this guideline will help you keep it useful for many years to come. Not only will you have fun with your family and friends; your children will enjoy the process too. Be proud and enjoy harvesting your produce multiple times during the year; it's your choice!

As you read through your copy of Hydroponics: The Beginner's Guide to Effective Hydroponic Gardening at Home, I hope you were able to use all of the handy tips provided. Whether you choose an indoor or outdoor version with a greenhouse; enjoy your creation. After all, Roman Emperor Tiberius enjoyed off-season cucumbers back in the

1st century AD; while becoming more popular in the 1600s.

Moving forward, the National Aeronautics & Space Administration (NASA) is using hydroponics for the astronauts. Think of Antarctica today being tested; who knows what's next? Maybe Mars.

As a keen gardener, what would be better than being able to do what you love, produce beautiful crops, and also make a profit from it! If this is something that you are interested in pursuing, with the right plan and mindset it's certainly something that you can achieve. Below are the key considerations you should make when planning to start a business from your hydroponic venture.

Check Your Local Demand and Market

The first thing you will need to determine is who would potentially be interested in buying your produce. Both local restaurants and markets are often looking for new suppliers of high quality produce. By investigating this market you will start to gain an idea of what is in demand and what you should grow. I suggest physically going out to communicate with restaurants and markets to identify some unique opportunities. It is always best to try pinpoint products that have a strong and stable demand - this will allow you to set a good price point. A prime example of this would be herbs such as basil. Fresh basil is always on the radar of good restaurants and it should be fairly straightforward to get interest for this culinary herb. On top of this, herbs require fairly little growing space and therefore easy to grow at large volumes - giving you a plentiful supply to fill the local demand!

At this stage it's also important to start looking into the legal requirements for starting a business in your area. This will likely prevent any administrative headaches in the future.

When exploring your local market start examining the selection of fresh herbs available, along with the level of the quality. Surprisingly enough, you will often many herbs that are below the standard that you could offer. It's a good idea to take note of both the quantities that are being sold and the pricing. Be sure to do conduct this informal research at a number of establishments, and you will then be able to compile this information to work out averages.

As I suggest starting your business with herbs, here is a list of some of the herbs that generally have the best demand and can be sold for a profitable price:

- Basil

- Oregano

- Mint

- French Tarragon

- French Sorrel

- Rosemary

- Dill

- Parsley

- Chive

- Sage

- Thyme

The Quality of Your Product

The most important factor for determining the success of your business is product quality. The great thing is that by growing hydroponically you can ensure that the quality of your products are top quality. I strongly suggest taking some time to perfect your hydroponic technique until you are able to get high quality results that are consistent. When you win your first clients, they will expect consistent results, and if you can deliver this your brand loyalty keep growing. On top of the quality of your produce, you will need to consider how your present your product. You will need to create product packaging that reflects the quality of your produce. As the saying goes, 'less is more' and you don't necessarily need sophisticated packaging - it is best to keep your costs down in the initial stages. You can simply use basic zip lock plastic bags with a sharp and clean label with your brand on. Make sure you make discreet breathing holes and apply a mist to your herbs before packaging them to maximize freshness.

www.ingramcontent.com/pod-product-compliance
Lightning Source LLC
Chambersburg PA
CBHW070907080526
44589CB00013B/1210